THE
ACCEPTABLE
SIN

Confronting the Cultural Imperative of Homosexuality

and the 21st-Century Church

THE
ACCEPTABLE
SIN

Confronting the Cultural Imperative of Homosexuality

and the 21st-Century Church

REDEMPTION
PRESS

WILLIAM HUCKABY

To contact the author, please email William@acceptablesin.com.

Published by Redemption Press, PO Box 427, Enumclaw, WA 98022.

Toll-Free (844) 2REDEEM (273-3336)

Redemption Press is honored to present this title in partnership with the author. The views expressed or implied in this work are those of the author. Redemption Press provides our imprint seal representing design excellence, creative content, and high-quality production.

ISBN: 978-1-64645-078-7 (Paperback)
978-1-64645-079-4 (ePub)
978-64645-080-0 (Mobi)

Library of Congress Catalog Card Number: 2020918214

CONTENTS

INTRODUCTION

Life Isn't Fair

ON OCTOBER 22, 2012, a low-pressure system formed in the southwestern Caribbean Sea just north of Panama. By the end of the day, the storm was upgraded to tropical storm status and was growing in intensity. Hurricane Sandy hit Cuba's shore on October 25, with sustained winds of 115 miles per hour. Classified as a category three hurricane, waves were recorded in excess of twenty-nine feet. When it departed Cuba's shores, it left behind more than $2 billion in damages and the loss of eleven souls.

The storm weakened in intensity, but even though the wind speed dropped it down into tropical storm status, the storm itself had grown in size. The National Hurricane Center later listed it as the largest hurricane to have ever formed in the Atlantic, having achieved a diameter of greater than one thousand miles—roughly three times the area of the state of Texas.

Because of its immense size, meteorologists came up with the nickname *Frankenstorm*, but it became more commonly known as *Super Storm*

Sandy. Sandy's sheer mass led to record-breaking storm tides along the East Coast, with New York recording tides of 13.9 feet, almost four feet higher than the previous record set back in 1960 by Hurricane Donna. One buoy off the coast of New York recorded a wave height of 32.5 feet, the largest there since records had been kept, and 6.5 feet higher than the previous record set by Hurricane Irene in 2011.

Simply put, it was a massive storm.

Sandy made landfall in New Jersey on the evening of October 29 and wreaked havoc over the northeastern United States for the next two days. Areas suffered flooding and a loss of gas and electricity. Gas rationing was instituted, and schools, airports, and hospitals were closed for days. It is estimated to have caused over $50 billion in damages, second only to Hurricane Katrina, with at least 147 American souls losing their lives.

In New Jersey, Richard and Elizabeth Everett were trying to make it home from their horse ranch with their two sons, Theo, fourteen, and Pierce, eleven, before the worst of the storm came on shore. They got as far as Mendham Township when a one-hundred-foot-tall, three-foot-wide tree was blown over onto the front of their truck cab, killing both parents instantly; the two boys sitting in the back seat escaped with only minor injuries.

The Everett's also had two daughters who were

not with them in the truck: seventeen-year-old Talia, and nineteen-year-old Zoe, who was beginning the adventure of her life as a freshman at Rutgers University forty miles away. On October 29, at eleven o'clock at night while studying for exams, Zoe received a phone call from her uncle that would forever change her life: both of her parents had been killed. Without hesitation she immediately left the college and battled through the storm to get back home to be with her younger siblings. Days later she announced she would abandon her hopes and dreams of college and would be leaving Rutgers to care for Talia, Theo, and Pierce. The Wish Upon a Hero website posted this statement about Zoe:

> She [Zoe] said she now has, "two goals: caring for and being guardian of my three younger siblings and keeping my family in the house we grew up in." Everett said after Hurricane Sandy, "I was no longer your typical nineteen-year-old. A moment in time, a second of bad luck, changed my life and my siblings' lives forever. I love them more than they could ever fathom and I am ready and willing to put any amount of weight on my shoulders to lessen the load on theirs. They are children who deserve to be kids and enjoy the

life they have lying before them. I am
going to be strong for them. I am going to be wise. I am going to be pa-
tient."[1]

There was a huge outpouring of financial support from their community and well beyond, but
no amount of money would change their situation:
their parents were still gone, and Zoe was the only
adult left to care for their family.

After reading about her situation and her in-
credibly courageous and selfless decision, I reflected
on the cards that life had dealt Zoe and her family,
and thought, *That isn't fair.*

Her attitude was certainly admirable, but didn't
Zoe also deserve to be a college kid as much as her
siblings deserved to just be kids?

To me, being fair is central to who I am. Several
years ago, I took the profile test offered through the
book *Strength Finder* [2] and discovered my number
one theme or strength is *consistency*. The results
defined consistency this way:

Balance is important to you. You are
keenly aware of the need to treat people the same, no matter what their
station in life, so you do not want to
see the scales tipped too far in any one
person's favor. This is truly offensive

to you. You see yourself as a guardian against it. In direct contrast to this world of special favors, you believe that people function best in a consistent environment where the rules are clear and are applied to everyone equally. This is an environment where people know what is expected. It is predictable and evenhanded. It is fair. Here each person has an even chance to show his or her worth.[3]

This explains why I find inconsistency or unfairness, especially to the extent dealt to the Everett family, and specifically to Zoe, to be offensive. My wife and I have frequently tried to prepare our children for life by teaching them that life isn't fair. But the immensity of Zoe's required sacrifice in the face of losing both parents seems extraordinarily cruel to me. It is all more than what one young woman alone should have to bear.

While we know by experience that life isn't fair, I believe there are institutions in our society that we have come to trust to be fair. Certainly, our justice system, which relies on our Constitution and the laws passed by our legislatures, believes itself to be fair. In almost every court of law in the United States, there is a statue of Lady Justice:

Figure 1: Lady Justice[4]

Lady Justice is more recognizable worldwide than the Statue of Liberty, as almost every courthouse on all seven continents exhibits her image. Her three main symbols are the blindfold, the sword, and the scales. These elements represent the fair and impartial administration of justice without influence by wealth, politics, popularity, greed, or corruption.

I think Christians in the North American church also believe themselves to be fair. Throughout history the church has been involved in many of the challenges facing society during its day. Very often the church has been a force for good, as its involvement has been central to the founding of many schools, hospitals, orphanages, and homeless shelters. It has also involved itself in moral issues, such as slavery, prohibition, abortion, and human trafficking. While abortion and human trafficking are still on the church's radar, it seems that the homosexual agenda and its attack on traditional, biblical family values is getting a considerable amount of our focus today.

I said *our focus*, as I count myself as part of the body of Christ, and, therefore, the church. In the year 2000, I was one who pushed back against the homosexual agenda with my involvement in the campaign for California's Proposition 22, known as the California Defense of Marriage Act, which simply stated: "Only marriage between a man and a woman is valid or recognized in California."[5]

Although the proposition passed easily with over 61 percent of the vote, there were many legal challenges to it, and it was repealed fifteen years later on January 1, 2015.

So, what happened?

You might remember in 1994, female comedian Ellen DeGeneres was the star of the sitcom *Ellen*. The show continued to grow in popularity and reached its height of success in 1997, the same year Ellen DeGeneres came out in an interview with Oprah Winfrey as being gay. Then in a two-part episode on the *Ellen* show, her character also came out as being gay. In response to Ellen and her character coming out, Jerry Falwell, a voice of the church at that time, referred to Ms. DeGeneres as "Ellen Degenerate." The show was canceled in 1998, presumably because of falling ratings due to the change in character and content in presenting a show centered on the first, openly homosexual character.

In 1998, society voted with its viewing choices.

Just five years later, in 2003, Ellen DeGeneres debuted on the television talk show *The Ellen DeGeneres Show*. At the time of this writing, Ms. DeGeneres has won twenty-nine Daytime Emmy Awards, twenty-one People's Choice Awards, and nine Teen Choice Awards for her work on the show.

In the last two decades, gay and lesbian relationships on television have become more mainstream, and celebrity-based homosexual relationships are more acceptable, certainly more than when *Ellen* was canceled in 1998 and when Proposition 22 was passed in 2000.

But how has the church responded to this societal reversal and the cultural war being waged? While continuing to be embroiled in the battle for traditional family values against the homosexual lifestyle, the church uses the Word of God as its standard to confront this sin. Utilizing the Bible as the plumb line, I believe the church makes every effort to resolve issues fairly, knowing their actions are often viewed by the world as representing the heart of God. In other words, what the world often believes about God is based upon what they see in the actions of the church. Whether the church is representing God to the world in an accurate, biblical, and loving way on this issue is another story.

The question I have is this: Is the church being fair?

I believe for far too long the church has addressed this very complicated subject one-dimensionally. To identify homosexuality as sin, which it is, and then base our response on this single issue is wrong because it ignores the more important truths of Christianity revealed to us through the life of Jesus.

That's what this book is all about.

Food for Thought:

1. The church has had some successes and failures in confronting the issues of the world. What has been your experience with the church being fair and unfair?

2. Has the church gone too far or not far enough when addressing the issues of the homosexual community? What could it do differently?

ONE

The Bible, the Church, and Moral Issues

All Scripture is inspired by God and is useful to teach us what is true and to make us realize what is wrong in our lives. It corrects us when we are wrong and teaches us to do what is right. God uses it to prepare and equip his people to do every good work.

2 Timothy 3:16–17 NLT

IN PAUL'S SECOND LETTER to Timothy, Paul explained to him that the writings in the Bible should be his standard for teaching people about the good news of Jesus Christ, and the basis for interpreting the events of the day.

Arguably most North American evangelical Christian churches would say the Bible is the foundation for their beliefs and blueprint for living. Because of this conviction, the church has involved itself in the moral issues challenging traditional Judeo-Christian values throughout history. Sometimes its involvement has been right on track; however, other times it missed the mark—the Crusades and Salem witch trials are obvious examples of this. Let's look at some more recent examples that have occurred over the last few hundred years.

Slavery

Although divided, some prominent North American church leaders spoke out against slavery. In 1774, John Wesley, the founder of Methodism, referred to slavery as "the sum of all villainies."[6] Charles Finney, a Presbyterian minister, believed slavery to be a moral sin. In his memoirs, he wrote of his attitude toward slavery during the early 1800s: "I had made up my mind on the question of slavery, and was exceedingly anxious to arouse public attention to the subject. In my prayers and preaching, I so often alluded to slavery, and denounced it."[7]

Finney firmly believed anyone who supported slavery after being enlightened on the subject would invite "the greatest guilt"[8] upon them.

Biblically speaking, the Bible gives guidelines for slaves and slave owners, but does not come out against the practice of slavery. However, the cruelty exercised over many of the slaves in the United States and United Kingdom, and the growing idea that slaves were not property but human beings and, therefore, deserved the rights of freedom and liberty—biblically based concepts—were probably the driving forces behind the abolitionist movement of the church.

Prohibition

Although, again divided, some denominations were the early leaders of the temperance movement of the 1800s and early 1900s. Their support of Prohibition was certainly tied to Paul's admonition to the church in Ephesus when he wrote, "Do not get drunk on wine, which leads to debauchery. Instead, be filled with the Spirit" (Ephesians 5:18 NIV).

However, the Bible itself does not specifically teach abstinence from alcoholic beverages; in fact, it permits the consumption of wine and strong drink during the celebration of bringing in the second tithe found in Deuteronomy. "You may spend the money for whatever your heart desires: for oxen, or sheep, or wine, or strong drink, or whatever your heart desires; and there you shall eat in the presence of the Lord your God and rejoice, you and your household" (Deuteronomy 14:26 NASB).

During the Last Supper with His disciples, Jesus even used wine as a symbol of the new covenant for His blood that was to be shed on the cross:

> Then he took a cup, and when he
> had given thanks, he gave it to them,

> saying, "Drink from it, all of you.
> This is my blood of the covenant,
> which is poured out for many for the
> forgiveness of sins. I tell you, I will
> not drink from this fruit of the vine
> from now on until that day when I
> drink it new with you in my Father's
> kingdom." (Matthew 26:27–29 NIV)

Although no clear denunciation can be found
in the Bible, I'm sure a strong motivation for some
denominations to press toward temperance was the
social ills tied to alcoholism. This was evident in
the early 1800s and the advent of the Industrial
Revolution, which brought increased drunkenness
that resulted in poverty, unemployment, crime,
and the destruction of the family.

Abortion

On January 22, 1973, abortion was legalized
in the United States by the Supreme Court. While
there is no clear mandate in the Bible prohibiting
abortion, the Bible, of course, speaks strongly
against murder. Divisions within the church
continue on the issue of abortion, however most
evangelical Christians would say they embrace the
sanctity of human life, and believe life begins at
conception, often using a verse from Psalms to
support this belief:

> You made all the delicate, inner parts
> of my body and knit me together in
> my mother's womb. Thank you for
> making me so wonderfully complex!
> Your workmanship is marvelous—
> how well I know it. You watched me
> as I was being formed in utter seclu-
> sion, as I was woven together in the
> dark of the womb. You saw me before
> I was born. Every day of my life was
> recorded in your book. Every moment
> was laid out before a single day had
> passed. (Psalm 139:13–16)

Since the Bible expresses that an unborn child
is a human life, abortion is considered murder. The
Bible also instructs Christians to be a voice for the
voiceless and to protect the vulnerable:

> Speak up for those who cannot speak
> for themselves, for the rights of all
> who are destitute. Speak up and judge
> fairly; defend the rights of the poor
> and needy. (Proverbs 31:8–9 NIV)

> Enough! You've corrupted justice long
> enough, you've let the wicked get away
> with murder. You're here to defend
> the defenseless, to make sure that
> underdogs get a fair break; Your job

is to stand up for the powerless, and
prosecute all those who exploit them.
(Psalm 82:2–4 MSG)

These verses and others like these prompt the church to be involved in bringing an end to the legal practice of abortion.

Homosexuality

While abortion has continued to be an issue within the church, the issue of homosexuality has grown increasingly prevalent in the last few decades. In contrast to the other social issues listed above, the Bible speaks more clearly and specifically against homosexuality than any other. Let me give you six biblical references: three from the Old Testament and three from the New Testament:

Old Testament

The first of these passages concerns Lot and the two male visitors, or angels, he received in Sodom:

But before they retired for the night, all the men of Sodom, young and old, came from all over the city and surrounded the house. They shouted to Lot, "Where are the men who came to spend the night with you? Bring them out to us so we can have sex with them!" So Lot stepped outside to talk to them, shutting the door behind him. "Please, my brothers," he begged, "don't do such a wicked thing. Look, I have two virgin daughters. Let me bring them out to you, and you can do with them as you wish. But please, leave these men alone, for they are my guests and are under my protection." "Stand back!" they shouted. "This fellow came to town as an outsider, and now he's acting like our judge! We'll treat you far worse than those other men!" And they lunged toward Lot to break down the door. But the two angels reached out, pulled Lot into the house, and bolted the door. Then they blinded all the men, young and old, who were at the door of the house, so they gave up trying to get inside. (Genesis 19:4–11)

Do not practice homosexuality, having sex with another man as with a woman. It is a detestable sin. (Leviticus 18:22 NIV)

If a man practices homosexuality, having sex with another man as with a woman, both men have committed a detestable act. They must both be put to death, for they are guilty of a capital offense. (Leviticus 20:13 NIV)

New Testament

But God shows his anger from heaven against all sinful, wicked people who suppress the truth by their wickedness. That is why God abandoned them to their shameful desires. Even the women turned against the natural way to have sex and instead indulged in sex with each other. And the men, instead of having normal sexual relations with women, burned with lust for each other. Men did shameful things with other men, and as a result of this sin, they suffered within themselves the penalty they deserved. (Romans 1:18, 26–27)

Don't you realize that those who do wrong will not inherit the Kingdom of God? Don't fool yourselves. Those who indulge in sexual sin, or who worship idols, or commit adultery, or are male prostitutes, or practice homosexuality, or are thieves, or greedy people, or drunkards, or are abusive, or cheat people—none of these will inherit the Kingdom of God. (1 Corinthians 6:9–10)

We know that the law is good when used correctly. For the law was not intended for people who do what is right. It is for people who are lawless and rebellious, who are ungodly and sinful, who consider nothing sacred and defile what is holy, who kill their father or mother or commit other murders. The law is for people who are sexually immoral, or who practice homosexuality, or are slave traders, liars, promise breakers, or who do anything else that contradicts the wholesome teaching that comes from the glorious Good News entrusted to me by our blessed God. (1 Timothy 1:8–11)

The church took a moral stand to confront and bring about an end to slavery, the sale of alcohol, and abortion. What is the church trying to accomplish over the societal issue of homosexuality? The Bible is clear that practicing homosexuality is a sin, but how should that fact define our approach to the people in the LGBTQ community?

Are we having a positive impact on them? Are we building bridges, or walls?

Food for Thought:

1. What do you think of the moral issues the church has chosen to confront throughout history?
2. Would you describe the church's approach to the homosexual as a success or a failure? Why?

TWO

The Church's Response to Homosexuals

THE TITLE OF THIS chapter is very specific. While it is one thing for the church to publicly proclaim its beliefs regarding the homosexual lifestyle, it should be another to discuss our response to *people* who are homosexual. Why? Because then we are putting faces to the issue. We're not talking about a group but, instead, about individuals with unique histories of experiences and feelings. Individuals are more vulnerable than a group. I believe Christians need to respond to gays and lesbians on a personal and relational level, in the same way Jesus calls us into a personal relationship with Him—but we don't often do this. We tend to lump all homosexual people into a group and have an *us* versus *them* mentality, which is detrimental to how the world perceives God's unconditional love for them—and perception is reality.

To get a feel for how North American religions and denominations stand on homosexuality, it is reasonable to look at how each of them responds to same-sex marriage. Pew Research recorded attitudes

toward same-sex marriage in major religious groups
as of July 2015.[9]

Support Same-Sex Marriage	Prohibit Same-Sex Marriage	No Clear Position
Conservative and Reformed Jewish Movements	National Baptist & Southern Baptist Conventions	Hinduism
Episcopal	American Baptist	Buddhism
Evangelical Lutheran	Roman Catholic	
Presbyterian	Assemblies of God	
Quaker	Mormon	
Unitarian	Orthodox Jewish	
United Church of Christ	United Methodist Churches	

Although United Methodists were listed in
the Pew Research article as prohibiting same-
sex marriage, the denomination is actually split
over the issue, and it has become a source of
division and conflict. While this research reveals
the denominational attitudes toward same-sex
marriage, it falls short in identifying how churches
who ban it from their practice respond to the
individual people themselves who are homosexual,
or part of the LGBTQ community. For instance,
do they welcome them to attend their services?

Can they become members of the church? Can they hold positions of leadership? Are they required to renounce their homosexuality before they can do any of these? Can they participate in church leadership if they are homosexual but remain celibate? Do they have to pronounce themselves free from same-sex attraction to be involved to any degree in church ministry?

No church would say its members and leaders are without sin, and the Bible makes that clear:

"If we claim we have no sin, we are only fooling ourselves and not living in the truth. If we claim we have not sinned, we are calling God a liar and showing that his word has no place in our hearts" (1 John 1:8, 10).

But most churches treat the sin of homosexuality differently than the other more *acceptable* sins committed by its members. So, what's the difference? Why are some sins overlooked or excused, while homosexuality is treated like Old Testament leprosy? Some have put forth the following three arguments about why the sin of homosexuality should be considered more offensive to the body of Christ.

1. It is a sexual sin.

Paul writes to the Corinthians, "Run from sexual sin! No other sin so clearly affects the body as this one does. For sexual immorality is a sin against your own body." (1 Corinthians 6:1)

Paul seems to differentiate the sin of sexual immorality—which encompasses homosexuality as we see from verse nine of the same chapter—from other sins because "it affects the body." In his instructions to "run from sexual sin," it would seem he believed those sins to be worse than other sins. In fact, he specifically states in verse nine, "none of these will inherit the Kingdom of God."

2. It is a lifestyle sin.

When the Holy Spirit convicts us of an area of sin in our lives, we typically feel regret and sorrow. We ask God to forgive us, and for His Holy Spirit to provide the strength to overcome the temptation. And if we've sinned against others, we ask for their forgiveness as well. We are promised that if we take these steps, He will forgive us. "But if we confess our sins to him, he is faithful and just to forgive us our sins and to cleanse us from all wickedness" (1 John 1:9).

In contrast, to live the homosexual lifestyle is to apparently not show any remorse. They feel no conviction or regret, as there is no obvious change in their actions. Simply put, there is no apparent effort to overcome their sin.

3. It is a sin that is celebrated.

Not only is there often no regret, it is a sin that is frequently celebrated. People who are caught in adultery don't then take to the streets and join a parade with other adulterers to show their pride in the actions they have taken, but many in the homosexual community do that very thing. Mike Goeke, former associate pastor of Stonegate Fellowship Church in Midland, Texas, who led Cross Power Ministries—a ministry for people struggling with unwanted same-sex attraction—said, "The truth is that homosexuality IS different. Homosexuality is the only sinful behavior that has a cultural identity and movement surrounding it. What other sin is encouraged to be celebrated? What other sin has a 'pride' movement attached to it?"[10]

Based on these arguments, I believe the church feels confident and comfortable in treating the sin of homosexuality differently than other sins that are more common within its walls.

But is the way we are treating homosexuals biblical? Are our actions pleasing to God? These are the questions we need to ask ourselves as Christians—as the church.

It has been my experience that people are much more tolerant of the sins they struggle with themselves, that is, those that are considered *common to man*, than they are of the sins they are not tempted by or may even find offensive. Let's take a closer look at this concept in the next chapter.

Food for Thought:

1. Have you witnessed the church using these arguments to justify how they treat the LGBTQ community?

2. What attitudes have you seen from your church toward gays and lesbians? What is your attitude?

THREE

The Acceptable Sin

IN APRIL OF 1994, Wisconsin minister Roy Ratcliff was called to the Columbia Correctional Institution because an inmate wanted to be baptized. He had no idea the prisoner's name was Jeffrey Dahmer.

Do you *remember* Jeffrey Dahmer? He was the infamous serial killer, who was eventually captured in 1991. Dahmer abducted, raped, tortured, murdered, and cannibalized his seventeen victims for sexual pleasure—all males between the ages of fourteen and thirty-three. Dahmer's defense by reason of insanity was rejected by his jury. He was found sane and was sentenced to prison for fifteen consecutive life sentences.[11]

[*WARNING: GRAPHIC DESCRIPTION OF HIS CRIMES FOLLOW IN THIS NEXT PARAGRAPH*]

When Dahmer's Milwaukee, Wisconsin, apartment was searched, it was found to be one of the most gruesome crime scenes ever discovered on record. Dahmer kept a photo album with pictures of his victims before their deaths, and his house was also found to contain their human remains after death and dismemberment. There were skulls, heads, extremities, and organs in his refrigerator and freezer, and in jars throughout the apartment. In the corner of his bedroom, police found a 57-gallon drum with bodies decomposing in a solution of muriatic acid. There was even evidence he had been eating some of his victims.[12]

Pastor Ratcliff, having lived in Wisconsin, was well aware of the atrocities Jeffrey Dahmer was convicted of committing. Yet believing God had called him to simply answer his phone that day, he chose to honor Dahmer's request and went to the prison to meet with him. Wanting to be sure of the sincerity of Dahmer's spiritual conversion before baptizing him, Pastor Ratcliff met and talked with him until he was convinced his repentance to be genuine and eventually performed the baptism.

When I heard the story of Jeffrey Dahmer's conversion, I thought, *Certainly not Jeffrey Dahmer. His crimes and actions were too heinous, too evil to even discuss. He showed no mercy to his victims, so he certainly doesn't deserve mercy and grace; he deserves justice.* I'm sure I was not alone in my thoughts.

After Dahmer's baptism, Ratcliff began traveling to the prison weekly to meet with Dahmer until he was murdered on November 28, 1994. In his book *Dark Journey Deep Grace*, Pastor Ratcliff records the most common question he receives when he tells people about his experience: *Was Jeffrey Dahmer sincere when he came to Christ?* His answer is always the same:

> Yes, I am convinced he was sincere. But this question bothers me. Why question the sincerity of another person's faith? The people asking me didn't know about his post-baptismal life. They were basing their question on what he did before he was baptized, not after. That bothers me. Jeff was judged not by his faith but by his crimes. The questioner always seemed to hope I'd answer: 'No, he wasn't sincere.' The questioner seemed to be looking for a way to reject Jeffrey as a brother in Christ instead of seeing him as a sinner who has come to God.
>
> They didn't want to think of Jeff as a brother.
>
> Was Jeff saved? Were his sins taken away? Was he a Christian believer? Did he repent of his sins? Did Jeff mean it when he said, "I'm so sorry for what I've done. God help me, I'll never do that again"? Or was the blood of Christ shed on the cross somehow too weak, too thin, too anemic to cover his sins?[13]

I would guess most of you find Jeffrey Dahmer's sins to be as offensive as I do. This is an easy example of not being tolerant of other people's sins; I'm sure almost 100 percent of you reading this book do not struggle with the same temptations he did. I'm just grateful the prison system reached out to someone like Pastor Ratcliff whose heart was much less judgmental and much more full of grace than mine. Because of the words and actions of Pastor Ratcliff, I am convicted that the crimson blood of Christ is *not* too weak, anemic, or thin to cover even Jeffrey Dahmer's sins.

While the sins of Jeffrey Dahmer are reprehensible to everyone, there are other sins practiced within the church that are far from that 100 percent threshold and hit a little closer to home. Let's take a look at some of these.

Pornography

While not exclusively a male problem, a recent study quoted by the *Huffington Post* said men are 543 percent more likely to look at pornography than women are.[14] Clearly this is a sin that men struggle with to a much greater degree than women. The same article quoted a Barna study that reported 64 percent of American males viewed porn at least monthly.

Perhaps more alarming is that the percentage of

Christian men who viewed porn at least monthly was virtually the same as non-Christian men.[15]

Another survey reported over half of surveyed, evangelical pastors admitted to viewing pornography in the last twelve months.[16] The problem with that statistic is that it only represents the pastors who were willing to admit to it in their survey, so the actual number could be higher. These are the leaders of our churches, our spiritual overseers.

Heterosexual pornography appeals to the male fantasy that sexually exploits and objectifies women for their mental and physical sexual pleasure. So, it is understandable why a majority of Christian women would find pornography offensive, and are unlikely to tolerate its use in any fashion by members of the church.

I once heard a radio interview many years back where a Christian man who struggled with pornography told the story of how he used to frequent his local convenience store several times a week for gas, snacks, and so forth, until the owner decided to start selling pornographic magazines. Not only was he selling them, he had them prominently on display. The man went to the manager and told him he was no longer going to be patronizing his store because of the pornography.

When the owner asked the man if his decision was because he found the magazines offensive, the man surprisingly told him *no*. He then explained that if the magazines were offensive to him, it would have been easy to continue to frequent the store and not be tempted by the publications on display. But it was because he *didn't* find them offensive, and was actually drawn to them, that he had to stop coming in. The owner, astonished by his customer's honest and transparent answer, completely understood why the man would not be returning.

The exploitation of women is not a new sin. The Bible has many stories that illustrate how this struggle is not unique to present-day men. Probably the most extreme and well-known is David's inability to turn his eyes away from the body of Bathsheba. His sin led to adultery and eventually to murder, as he attempted to cover up his moral failure. David was the leader of the Jewish nation, a man who had multiple wives and concubines (think slaves or mistresses), and the one who God later declared was a man after His own heart.

It is easy to understand why most women find pornography offensive, and can't comprehend the draw it has on the male mind (and if we are honest, every male mind, Christian or not). But it also makes sense men would be more forgiving, and would extend a greater degree of mercy and grace to those found to be in pornography, because it is a sin they struggle with as well—a sin they understand and have yielded to.

The sins of Jeffrey Dahmer are offensive to everyone, while the sin of pornography is offensive to most women, but understandable, and even tempting to most men.

Let's look at one more sin, the *acceptable* sin:

Gluttony

Proverbs has a lot to say about the sin of gluttony.

> Do not join those who drink too much wine or gorge themselves on meat, for drunkards and gluttons become poor, and drowsiness clothes them in rags. (Proverbs 23:20–21 NIV)

> He who keeps the law is a discerning son, but he who is a companion of gluttons humiliates his father. (Proverbs 28:7 NIV)

> And put a knife to your throat if you are given to gluttony. (Proverbs 23:2 NIV)

Gluttony is recognized by church tradition as one of the seven deadly sins, while temperance, or self-control—the antithesis of gluttony—is listed in the Bible as a virtue or fruit of the Spirit

(Galatians 5:22–23).

The Centers for Disease Control (CDC) uses body mass index (BMI) as the measurement for underweight, normal weight, overweight, obesity, and extreme/severe obesity (there is no measurement defined as *glutton*). You can easily find an online calculator to determine your BMI to see where you fall within their definition.

Body Mass Index (BMI)[17]

Underweight	BMI < 18.5
Normal Weight	BMI 18.5–25
Overweight	BMI 25–30
Obese	BMI > 30
Extreme/Severe Obesity	BMI > 40

The CDC reports that more than 70 percent of adult Americans are considered overweight, while more than 37 percent of American adults are considered obese.[18]

A surprising fact reported by a study from Purdue University found: "Religious people are more likely to be overweight than are nonreligious people."[19]

The Southern Baptist Convention confirmed similar findings in an Executive Summary Report of Wellness Center statistics from their 2005 convention. The report showed more than 75 percent of the 1,472 participants were found to be significantly overweight.[20]

The Bible describes the practice of gluttony as a sin, and yet this sin is rampant throughout the church, for both males and females, at epidemic proportions. In most cases, there is no correction from the pulpit or limitations on involvement in leadership put upon those embroiled in this sinful practice.

Few church members find this sin offensive. Why? Because many of those within the church, both men and women, struggle with it and are therefore more tolerant of it.

In the previous chapter, we listed three arguments Christians sometimes use to characterize the sin of homosexuality differently than other sins within the church. Let's now compare gluttony according to the same characteristics and see if they also apply.

1. Homosexuality is a sexual sin.

Paul warns the Corinthians to "run from sexual sin! No other sin so clearly affects the body as this one does" (1 Corinthians 6:18). While gluttony is not a sexual sin, does that mean it is a more acceptable sin in God's eyes than homosexuality?

Paul continues in the same verse to say, "For sexual immorality is a sin against your own body" (1 Corinthians 6:18). The CDC reports obesity-related conditions include heart disease, stroke, type 2 diabetes, and certain types of cancer—*some of the leading causes of preventable death*.[21] While gluttony is not a sexual sin, it clearly affects the body.

First Corinthians chapter 1 also includes the verse the church so often uses to tell Christians why smoking is a sin, since nowhere in the Bible does it speak out specifically against it: "Don't you realize that your body is the temple of the Holy Spirit, who lives in you and was given to you by God? You do not belong to yourself, for God bought you with a high price. So you must honor God with your body" (1 Corinthians 6:19–20).

Just like smoking, and perhaps more so, gluttony is a sin against your own body. It destroys the temple of the Holy Spirit and is a visible example of not honoring God. In verse 12 of the same passage, Paul admonishes the Corinthians not to become a slave to anything. The fact is, if you are a glutton, you are a slave to food.

2. Homosexuality is a lifestyle sin; so is gluttony.

You don't become obese by overindulging in just one meal. Obesity is the result of overindulging in many meals, perhaps all meals. It is the outcome of a lifestyle of making poor choices to gratify our flesh.

Repentance of sin is made up of two components:

having regret or remorse for the sin we've committed, and then turning from evil toward good. While we may regret being overweight, we don't seem to regret it enough to change. Most often we don't turn from the *evil* of gluttony, and turn towards the *good* to practice the self-control and denial of its temporary pleasures. Is that any different than homosexuals who don't repent?

3. Homosexuality is a sin that is celebrated.

In the last chapter, I quoted Mike Goeke as saying, "Homosexuality is the only sinful behavior that has a cultural identity and movement surrounding it." I would disagree. No culture celebrates the sin of gluttony more than the church. Think of your own church culture and the focal point of its social gatherings. In the churches I've attended, they have centered things around doughnuts, potlucks, bake sales, chili cook-offs, and carnivore nights for men's groups. The church is to gluttons what an open bar is to Alcoholics Anonymous and Celebrate Recovery groups. That might seem harsh, but it's true.

So, what's the difference between the sin of homosexuality and gluttony? Gluttony is accepted in the church, even celebrated, presumably because so many within the church struggle with it. Few dare to speak out or point a finger at it. Why is this a problem?

In Titus 1 and 1 Timothy 3, Paul outlines the qualifications for being an elder, or church leader, within the church body. In both descriptions, depending on the translation, he includes that they *must*:

Exercise self-control
Live a disciplined life
Be temperate

These qualifications are all defined as showing moderation or self-restraint. A glutton lacks these required characteristics, and yet a study from Baylor University indicates more than a third of the American clergy are obese.[22] More than a third of our pastors struggle with the sin of gluttony, and yet we ignore one of Paul's requirements for church leadership because most of us understand and are sympathetic to that struggle.

Here is the question: Why is the church's attitude toward the homosexual different than its attitude toward the glutton?

It is because *gluttony is the acceptable sin?*

In his letter to the Philippians, Paul warns them:

> For I have told you often before, and
> I say it again with tears in my eyes,
> that there are many whose conduct
> shows they are really enemies of the

> cross of Christ. They are headed for
> destruction. Their god is their *appetite*,
> they brag about shameful things, and
> they think only about this life here on
> earth. (Philippians 3:18–19, emphasis
> added)

In the New Living Translation version of the Bible, the Greek word **κοιλία *(koilia)*** translates as "appetite." The word *appetite* is a broad term in the English language but is often associated with food. However, *appetite* could also be interpreted as "craving" or "desire" and, therefore, applied as a sexual appetite (homosexuality, adultery, fornication, pornography, and so forth), or an appetite for material things (greed). It is clear by what Paul writes in the remainder of verse 19 that he is referring to those who are more focused on the pleasures of this world.

As a glutton, it is easy to then gloss over what Paul may have been specifically making a reference to in his letter to the Philippians. Let's look at what other translations of verse 19 say:

> Their destiny is destruction, their god
> is their *stomach*, and their glory is
> in their shame. Their mind is set on
> earthly things. (NIV, emphasis added)

> Their end is destruction, their god
> is their *belly*, and they glory in their
> shame, with minds set on earthly
> things. (ESV, emphasis added)

The Greek word **κοιλία (koilia)** is used ten times in the New Testament: four times to refer to the female abdomen or womb by doctor Luke (1:41, 44; 2:21; 11:27), three times to refer to the stomach (1 Corinthians 6:13, Revelation 10:10), and once to refer to the belly, or stomach, of a fish (Matthew 12:40).

It certainly appears there is high probability, when Paul was referring to the appetite of those headed for destruction in Philippians 3:19, he was referring to the anatomical stomach, rather than to evil desires. If nothing else, it certainly would include the excessive desire for food and gluttony.

You might remember one of the Old Testament references I used in chapter 2 to show how the Bible recognizes homosexuality as sin in the story of Sodom, but here is what God said through His prophet Ezekiel: "Sodom's sins were pride, *gluttony*, and laziness, while the poor and needy suffered outside her door. She was proud and committed detestable sins, so I wiped her out, as you have seen" (Ezekiel 16:49–50, emphasis mine).

When the church thinks of the story of Sodom,

we think of their *detestable sins* as specifically homosexuality. But gluttony was number two on God's list of their transgressions, while homosexuality isn't even mentioned.

Sobering isn't it? I don't know how many times I've read through that verse and didn't see, or didn't want to see, the omission of homosexuality from it. It makes me wonder what other teachings we as the church have overlooked in order to build our case of judgment against people who struggle with sins that are different from our own—a judgment that keeps us with our sin safely in the *saved* column, while ensuring those *other* people are pushed into the u*nsaved* column, and therefore excluded from the church.

Gluttony is a sin. Not a minor sin but a sin that Paul said shows we are enemies of the cross of Christ and headed for destruction, just like someone who is homosexual—those we so quickly point a finger at.

This realization should cause us to reevaluate how we as the church treat the LGBTQ community. Do we treat the individual who practices the sin of homosexuality the same as the person who practices the sin of gluttony?

Food for Thought:

1. Before reading this chapter, had you ever asked

yourself why the church seems to turn a blind
eye to the sin of gluttony?

2. As you have examined the sin in your own life,
   have you found that you compare your sins to
   the sins of others?

FOUR

Hate the Sin, Love the Sinner

IN THE EARLY MORNING hours of June 12, 2016, a twenty-nine-year-old security guard named Omar Mateen killed forty-nine people and wounded fifty-three others at a gay nightclub called Pulse in Orlando, Florida. The church response that got the most media coverage in the area I live was a quote from the pastor of a small Baptist church in Sacramento, California. In excerpts from his Sunday-night sermon, less than twenty-four hours after the shooting, he said,

> Are you sad that fifty pedophiles (*he believes all homosexuals are also pedophiles*) were killed today? Um—no—I think that's great! I think that helps society. I think Orlando, Florida, is a little safer tonight. We don't need to do anything to help. As far as I'm concerned, Orlando is a little bit safer tonight. I wish the government would round them all up, put them up against a firing wall, put a firing squad in front of them and blow their brains out.[23]

While his opinion certainly did not represent most of the churches in our region, it was the one that received the most press coverage, both local and national, and the one I'm sure the homosexual community of our region believes was representative of the attitude of the Christian church—hardly a fine moment for the church.

You often hear Christians recite the mantra, "Hate the sin, love the sinner." But I think as a Church we really suck at it in practice, especially toward those whose sins are on the outside looking in. Often the message communicated to the homosexual community is "hate the sin, hate the sinner," because many in the church judge them as perverse, depraved, unnatural, deviant, debased, degenerate, warped, twisted, corrupt, abnormal, unhealthy, immoral, wicked, vile, aberrant, evil, debauched, and amoral.

But in Luke 7:34 Jesus tells us the Pharisees referred to Him as a *friend of sinners*, because He could be found eating and drinking with tax collectors and the other disreputable people of His day (Matthew 9:10, Luke 15:1–2, Luke 19:7). Now it doesn't surprise me at all to find Jesus in the company of sinners, because He said He came to seek and save the lost (Luke 19:10), and He made it clear it isn't the healthy who need a physician but, rather, those who are sick (Mark 2:17).

What does surprise me is that these *notorious* sinners would want to hang out with Jesus. To think of it in modern-day terms, if I owned an adult bookstore or worked in human trafficking, the last person I would want to be in the presence of would be the Son of God; yet we read the exact opposite to be true.

There was something about the character of Jesus that drew the worst of the worst to Him. Even though Jesus never condoned sin, they felt drawn to His presence and wanted to listen to what He had to say; they felt the love behind His message. It seems to me if the Church is supposed to be Jesus to the world of today, and we are doing it effectively, then all sinners—regardless of their particular sin—would feel comfortable coming through the doors of our churches, and would feel God's love in the presence of fellow sinners.

But do they?

Here is the truth:

Homosexuals are not our enemies; Satan is the Enemy. Those who are part of the LGBTQ community are the potential casualties of this war against the "evil rulers and authorities of the unseen world, against mighty powers in this dark world, and against evil spirits in the heavenly places" (Ephesians 6:12).

We need to remind ourselves, we are not better

than they are, because we have all "fallen short of the glory of God," (Romans 3:23), and God loves them as much as He loves us. And as I type this paragraph, it saddens me that I am referring to the relationship between the gay community and God's church as "them" and "us," when God has created us all equal. Yet there does seem to be a great divide: an us versus them mentality.

Do we hate the sin of homosexuality and love the person who is homosexual in the same way we hate the sin of gluttony and love the glutton?

As a church, we need to examine what it really means to hate the sin but love the sinner, and try to do a better job of it when it comes to the gay community.

In the next chapter I will share with you my experience with the church, and my personal struggle with sin.

Food for Thought:

1. On a scale of 1–10, how would you rate the church on hating the sin of homosexuality and loving the sinner?

2. On a scale of 1–10, how would you rate yourself?

FIVE

People Who Live in
Glass Houses

WHEN READING MY ARGUMENT in support of homosexuals in the church, you might expect me to now tell you that I am a Christian and a homosexual . . . but that is not the case.

I have been married to a beautiful, godly woman for thirty-nine years, and we have four grown boys. That fact may lead you to think, "His poor wife, married to a man for thirty-nine years, and now he decides to come out of the closet. How horrible for his four grown sons to discover the truth about their father so late in life." No, I don't struggle with homosexuality, yet I am intimately involved in this discussion.

You see, I am a glutton and have been my entire life.

I have struggled with my weight since elementary school. I used to be the fastest kid in my first-grade class (sorry, Mark Dosher), but now I am six feet, three inches tall, and at my heaviest I weighed 333 pounds, with a BMI of 42: extremely obese.

Although I've had seasons of success dropping my weight down to 240 pounds a couple of times in my adult life, I have unsuccessfully been able to keep the weight off. When I turned fifty, my wife and I decided it was time for me to do something more serious than Weight Watchers, Nutrisystem, Atkins, Medifast, or a doctor-monitored weight-loss program where I was prescribed amphetamines. I qualified for bariatric surgery and opted for a lap band. After surgery I successfully lost ninety-three pounds.

But then I learned how to cheat.

At the time of this writing, I am back up to 285 pounds with a BMI of 35.6, which is still obese. I am, sadly, a committed glutton. Even though I have never successfully beaten my sin of gluttony, I have served as a board member at a Christian high school, held elder and lead elder positions at my church, led Bible studies and home groups, and even taught sermons in our Sunday services.

But how can that be possible?

I mean, if we use the Bible as our plumb line for decisions and direction within the church, then I am woefully unqualified. As I mentioned before, Paul's letters to Timothy and Titus give specific qualifications for those who hold positions of leadership within the church. Paul expressly lists the positions of elder and deacon, but I believe it is safe to apply these requirements to any leadership position in the church, including the senior pastor. Let me remind you, Paul specifies that individuals are to lead *disciplined* lives, be *temperate*, and *exhibit self-control* in order to be appointed to these positions. Clearly gluttons, such as myself, lack all three qualifications, yet the church turns a blind eye to such an obvious, biblically defined character flaw, while using what one author refers to as the *clobber verses* to reject and exclude homosexuals.

Is the church being fair?

I feel guilty and ashamed my sin is so quickly overlooked and accepted within the church, allowing me to not only attend services and be an active member, but also to hold positions of leadership. Indeed, most churches are a safe harbor for gluttons. To judge the sin of gluttony in many cases would mean to judge one's self; something those of us on the inside looking out are reluctant to do. So, we choose to ignore and justify it as we are in good company, since obesity is virtually epidemic within our walls. On the other hand, homosexuals are labeled as sexual deviants and ostracized by our churches to keep them on the outside of our safe, little, self-righteous club.

This is often referred to as a "double standard."

Some might say, and rightly so, even though God sees all sin as the same, the consequences of sin differ. For example, pastor and author John Piper said:

> First, not everybody is hurt in the same way by every sin. In other words, if I shoot Michael dead right now, or if I just spit on him, both are very ugly sins and Jesus calls hatred murder. But he's not dead if I only spit on him! So worse sin—meaning worse in its effect—would be killing over spitting. And I think we should say that. It is! Because consequences matter.[24]

Billy Graham echoed a similar thought:

> It is always difficult and dangerous to attempt to list sins according to their degree of seriousness. In one sense, all sins are equal in that they all separate us from God. The Bible's statement, 'For the wages of sin is death' (Romans 6:23), applies to all sin, whether in thought, word, or deed.
>
> At the same time, it seems obvious that some sins are worse than others in both motivation and effects and should be judged accordingly. Stealing a loaf of bread is vastly different than

exterminating a million people. Sins
may also differ at their root.

Theologians have sought for
centuries to determine what the
essence of sin is. Some have chosen
sensuality, others selfishness, and still
others pride or unbelief. In the Old
Testament, God applied different
penalties to different sins, suggesting
variations in the seriousness of some
sins."[25]

Acknowledging that some sins are more serious
and carry greater consequences than others, the
church is then quick to quantify homosexuality
as a worse sin than gluttony. However, in grading
the seriousness of sins, it would seem that John
Piper and Billy Graham believed at least one
criterion for doing so would include how the
sin affects or impacts others. The sin of murder
takes the life of another. Infidelity, adultery, and
divorce destroy families, spouses, and children. In
most situations, gluttony affects only the glutton
in the same way a person who is homosexual in a
monogamous relationship affects only the person
who is homosexual.

If we are honest, gluttony is not the only
acceptable sin within the church. While sexual

immorality includes homosexuality, it is a broad term, and there are those within the church walls who would be found guilty of some of its other expressions. The Bible also speaks against those who are quick to anger, the proud, the critical, gossips, and those enslaved to materialism—all of whom we recognize within the rank and file of our church membership.

Let's take a closer look at just two of those *acceptable* sins I believe are often ignored.

Materialism

If we look back at the history of the Bible and God's frustrated relationship with the Jews, we often see that the breaking point for God—when God would allow the Jews to be defeated, captured, enslaved, with their cities often destroyed—happened when His children chose to worship foreign gods and embrace idolatry. This certainly seemed to be a deal breaker for God, as the first two commandments relate to our faithfulness to Him and not to worship idols, and God has always described Himself as a jealous God. If we were looking for one sin that was worse than the others, I would say idolatry is certainly at the top of the list. Paul warns of idolatry in his letter to the Colossians: "Don't be greedy, for a greedy person is an idolater, worshiping the things of this world" (Colossians 3:5).

Greed = idolatry

Thesaurus.com lists the word *greedy* as the number one synonym for the term *materialistic*.[26] Greed, materialism, and covetousness are all closely intertwined, and Paul proclaims these as a form of idolatry—a major offense against a jealous God. But Paul expands further in his letter to the Ephesians when he puts greed on par with sexual immorality or homosexuality: "Let there be no sexual immorality, impurity, or greed among you. Such sins have no place among God's people" (Ephesians 5:3).

Paul then goes on to warn the Ephesians: "You can be sure that no immoral, impure, or greedy person will inherit the Kingdom of Christ and of God. For a greedy person is an idolater, worshiping the things of this world" (Ephesians 5:5).

Did you catch that? Paul lumps together those who are greedy and worship the things of the world with people who are homosexual, and he tells us they will not inherit the kingdom of God.

Paul also gives the same instructions to the Colossians: "So put to death the sinful, earthly things lurking within you. Have nothing to do with sexual immorality, impurity, lust, and evil desires. Don't be greedy, for a greedy person is an idolater, worshiping the things of this world. Because of these sins, the anger of God is coming" (Colossians 3:5–6).

I have a friend, a Nazarene pastor, who told me that in the 1940s and 1950s, some members of the Nazarene churches wouldn't have wedding rings. Why? Because they believed that was money that could be devoted to the kingdom of God.

Personally, I believe a wedding ring is an important symbol that shows the world my commitment to my wife, hopefully modeling Jesus's commitment to His church. But I wonder what the Nazarenes of that day would have thought if they just looked at the parking lots of today's North American Church?

I have no problem with the wealthy, as I believe it is God who has chosen to bless (curse?) them with their ability to make money. The Bible is filled with individuals whom God chose to bless with material possessions, but the issue is what they did with their wealth. Jesus says in Luke, "From everyone who has been given much, much will be demanded; and from the one who has been entrusted with much, much more will be asked" (12:48).

We need to be careful not to judge the wealthy by their possessions, but by their generosity—what they do with their wealth. Do they use their blessings to improve their standard of living only, or to improve their standard of giving?

Paul gave Timothy these instructions when he was serving at the church in Ephesus:

> Teach those who are rich in this world not to be proud and not to trust in their money, which is so unreliable. Their trust should be in God, who richly gives us all we need for our enjoyment. Tell them to use their money to do good. They should be rich in good works and generous to those in need, always being ready to share with others. By doing this they will be storing up their treasure as a good foundation for the future so that they may experience true life. (1 Timothy 6:17–19)

Dosomething.org reports, "Nearly half of the world's population, more than 3 billion people, live on less than $2.50 a day. More than 1.3 billion live in extreme poverty, living on less than $1.25 a day. 80% of the world population lives on less than $10.00 a day."[27]

Eighty percent of the world lives on less than $300 a month! Can you imagine? I don't think it is unreasonable to say, at least by the world's standards, the sin of materialism is rampant within the American church, maybe even epidemic—and it affects me as well. But are the materialistic (greedy) welcome in our churches? John warns,

"Do not love the world or the things in the world. If anyone loves the world, the love of the Father is not in him" (1 John 2:15 ESV).

Do the greedy—idolaters—hold positions of leadership in our churches even when the Bible tells us the love of the Father is not in them? Does your church treat those who struggle with the sin of materialism (greed/covetousness), the same as those who are homosexual?

Sexual Immorality

Let me ask you this: What exactly is sexual immorality? From the Greek *por·nei'a*, it is a general term for all unlawful sexual intercourse, which includes prostitution (sex for money), fornication (sexual relations between unmarried individuals), adultery (sexual relations between married individuals not married to each other), homosexuality, and bestiality (I'd rather not define this).

Let's examine, specifically, adultery within the church.

While I realize some churches do not allow individuals who have gone through divorce to hold positions of leadership, many do not attach that restriction. Hypothetically speaking, let's look at a potential story of adultery within the church (we'll make the husband the bad guy).

Craig and Melinda have been attending

Springfield Community Church regularly since they got married eleven years ago. They now have two young children, and Melinda is a stay-at-home mom volunteering weekly in their children's Sunday school class.

Craig's eyes begin to wander to a single woman at work named Heather, who attends the same church. They sometimes eat lunch together and linger in the parking lot at the end of the day, and Craig makes every effort to have Heather placed on his project team at work. Craig feels that Heather, who is very easy on the eyes, really listens to him, respects his work, laughs at his jokes, and seems to enjoy spending time with him. Craig begins to pursue Heather, but he doesn't have to work very hard, as Heather is drawn to Craig even though she knows he is married with two children. They begin to talk more openly, even acknowledging that what they are doing is wrong, but they make each other *happy*. Certainly, God wants them to be *happy*, right?

Craig and Heather decide they want to spend the rest of their life together, so Craig goes home and packs a bag and tells Melinda he is leaving her to be with Heather. Melinda contacts the church and tells them what Craig is doing. The pastor reaches out to Craig and meets him for lunch to listen to his explanation, and to talk with him about the sanctity of marriage and the covenant he made before God when he married Melinda. Craig listens to his pastor, but tells him Heather makes him happy and he is sticking by his decision to be with her. The pastor explains to Craig that if he is unwilling to try and reconcile with Melinda, and is determined to stay on the path he has chosen, he and Heather will have to leave the church. Craig understands but is unmoved. The pastor tells Craig he will be praying for him and how sorry he is to see Craig's marriage to Melinda destroyed.

Fast-forward eighteen months later when Craig and Melinda's divorce is final, and Craig and Heather are now able to get married. They have a small, civil ceremony and begin their life together. A few months into the marriage, they both discover they miss the community of the church. They know their decision to be together was a violation of God's perfect will, so they ask God to forgive them and to bless them as their marriage goes forward. They find a church home at Franklin Community Church, and meet with the pastor to explain what has transpired over the last two years. The pastor receives them into his church to help restore their relationship with God, because the Bible promises, "If we confess our sins, he is faithful and just to forgive us our sins and to cleanse us from all unrighteousness" (1 John 1:9 ESV).

He is the God of second chances.

Craig and Heather really enjoy the people of Franklin Community Church and quickly begin to develop friendships with some of the other members. Heather is asked if she would be willing to assist in the second-grade Sunday school class, and Craig is asked if he would serve as an usher once a month. Heather soon becomes the permanent first-grade Sunday school teacher, while Craig becomes the lead usher, and then he is asked if he would be willing to serve on the deacon board. Craig and Heather love God and stay connected to each other and their church until they each die of old age.

The end.

Using the test of time, Craig and Heather certainly seemed repentant and turned their lives around. But what does the Bible say about divorce? When Jesus was asked the question of divorce, He explains in Matthew 19:8 that though Moses allowed divorce because of their "hardness of heart," it is not part of God's original plan for marriage. Jesus also says this regarding divorce:

> But I say to you that everyone who divorces his wife, except on the ground of sexual immorality, makes her commit adultery, and whoever marries a divorced woman commits adultery. (Matthew 5:32 ESV)

And I say to you: whoever divorces his
wife, except for sexual immorality, and
marries another, commits adultery.
(Matthew 19:9 ESV)

While Jesus didn't say divorce is a sin, He did
say (with one exception) if you divorce and remarry,
or if you marry a divorced person, you commit
adultery—which is understood to be a sin of sexual
immorality (like homosexuality). To understand
why marriage after divorce would be considered
adultery, I think we need to look at what God told
the Israelites through the prophet Malachi:

You cry out, "Why doesn't the Lord
accept my worship?" I'll tell you
why! Because the Lord witnessed the
vows you and your wife made when
you were young. But you have been
unfaithful to her, though she remained
your faithful partner, the wife of your
marriage vows. Didn't the Lord make
you one with your wife? In body and
spirit you are his. So guard your heart;
remain loyal to the wife of your youth.
"For I hate divorce!" says the Lord, the
God of Israel. "To divorce your wife
is to overwhelm her with cruelty,"
says the Lord of Heaven's Armies. "So

guard your heart; do not be unfaithful
to your wife." (Malachi 2:14–16)

That's a pretty serious indictment, isn't it? Yet
divorce and remarriage are commonplace in our
society today—including in the church. I believe
the reason Jesus considered remarriage after divorce
to be adultery was because even though the state
you reside in grants divorce and allows a divorcee
to remarry, God doesn't recognize an individual as
being divorced just because the state says they are.

Jesus said as much when He described the
marriage relationship in God's eyes:

> He answered, "Have you not read
> that he who created them from the
> beginning made them male and female,"
> and said, "Therefore a man shall leave
> his father and his mother and hold fast
> to his wife, and the two shall become
> one flesh"? So they are no longer two
> but one flesh. What therefore God has
> joined together, let not man separate."
> (Matthew 19:4–6 ESV)

When Craig left Melinda for Heather, Craig
and Heather were committing adultery. Jesus's
words in the Bible make it clear that when Craig and

Heather got married, they were also committing adultery.

Ask yourself these questions:

At what point in their second marriage relationship are they not committing adultery?

When does their marriage cease being adultery?

Does it ever?

I don't have the answers to these questions, but it is worthy of discussion in the body of Christ. It doesn't seem fair that after a certain amount of time the church welcomes back a couple who is in a lifestyle of adultery, a form of sexual immorality, but rejects and excludes somebody who is gay or lesbian.

Why do so many of us work to make same-sex marriage illegal, but wouldn't consider doing the same with divorce? Jesus never references homosexuality in the Bible, but speaks out very strongly against divorce, as did His Father. "'For I hate divorce!' says the Lord, the God of Israel" (Malachi 2:16).

Let's not stop there but expand our characterization of adultery within the church to include what Jesus said about adultery, "'You have heard the commandment that says, 'You must not commit adultery.' But I say, anyone who even looks at a woman with lust has already committed adultery with her in her heart.'" (Matthew 5:27–28)

On any given summer day in California, when

female clothing is at a minimum, many Christian males could be found guilty of adultery by what they see and think to themselves. If you expand that to include pornography, which over half of surveyed evangelical pastors admitted to viewing in the last year, then by Jesus's standards, clearly a majority of Christian men could be found guilty of adultery—yet they are not subjected to the same limitations as homosexuals.

Geoffrey Chaucer writes, "People who live in glass houses should not throw stones."[28]

The Cambridge Dictionary explains the meaning of the idiom as, "This means that you should not criticize other people for bad qualities in their character that you have yourself."[29]

Yet many of us who make up the body of Christ live in glass houses, don't we? I shared with you at the beginning of this book how important being fair is to me, but I realize it may not be as important for you. However, doesn't the church, and we as Christians, have a responsibility to be fair to every individual whom God loves and comes through our doors? I believe we do.

I'm not saying homosexuality is not sin; the Bible is clear it is. I am saying gluttony, pride, materialism (idolatry), gossiping, lust, a critical spirit, adultery (including cases of divorce), and more are also sins. So why do we treat homosexuality differently?

James, the brother of Jesus, told us, "For the person who keeps all of the laws except one is as guilty as a person who has broken all of God's laws" (James 2:10).

I am a glutton. Therefore, I am as guilty as a greedy person, adulterer, and/or the person who is homosexual. Shouldn't I be treated the same? Shouldn't I be held to the same standard and restrictions as a gay or lesbian? Having a double standard for the sins that are more common in our churches isn't fair.

Shouldn't the person who is homosexual be allowed the same opportunities the church has granted me?

That would be fair.

Food for Thought:

1. While many of us may be friends with couples who are divorced and remarried as a result of adultery in their past, I think few of us could count a homosexual in our rank of friends. Being honest, do you view or treat the sin of homosexuality differently than the sin of your friends who are divorced and remarried?

2. In truth, not just many of us in the church live in glass houses; all of us do. What sins in your life have built the walls of your glass house?

SIX

Understanding the Homosexual

I DON'T. UNDERSTAND THE homosexual, that is.

But then again, I never tried to.

I understand gluttony, materialism, and lust, but not same-sex attraction. I had always just assumed there was something wrong with homosexuals for making that *choice*.

As God started to convict me of the logs within my own eye (Matthew 7:3), I began to do some research. I am not qualified to explain the challenge of the person who is homosexual, but perhaps I can provide some resources that may give you a better understanding; I know they helped me.

The first book I read on the topic was *Stranger at the Gate: To Be Gay and Christian in America*, by Mel White. I was led to this book through a blog I read on Phil Yancey's website. Mel was actively involved in the evangelical Protestant movement (religious right) and was a pastor and professor at Fuller Theological Seminar. He was a ghostwriter for Pat Robertson, Jerry Falwell, and Billy Graham, and he also wrote Christian film and television specials. Mel was married to Lyla and the father of two children.

Mel was also attracted to men.

Believing same-sex attraction was a sin and not compatible with his Christian faith, he attempted many *cures* for what he believed to be a mental illness. He reasoned that if he married a good woman, those homosexual desires would fall away. He did find and marry a great woman, but nothing changed in his heart. He shared his struggle with others and asked for prayer, and then engaged in psychotherapy without success. Finally, in desperation, he submitted himself to extreme treatments, including exorcism and electroconvulsive therapy, also known as shock treatment.

Two things were clear to me in reading his book:

1. He wanted more than anything to be free from these same-sex desires; he yearned to be heterosexual.
2. He was willing to do anything to be set free.

As badly as he wanted to be *normal* in his sexual desires, nothing worked. After attempting suicide, Mel and his wife agreed to an amicable divorce, with his ex-wife even writing the foreword to his book.

Philip Yancey posted an interview on his blog where he addressed his friendship with Mel:

> I don't agree with some of Mel's choices, but they are Mel's choices, not mine, and thus between Mel and God. I think back to Jesus and how offensive he must have found the people he dealt with; yet he treated them with respect, compassion, and love.
>
> On an issue like this, I try to start with what I'm absolutely sure of and work outwards. I'm sure of what my own attitude should be toward gays and lesbians: I should show love and grace. As one person told me, "Christians get very angry toward other Christians who sin differently than they do." When people ask me how I can possibly stay friends with a sinner like Mel, I respond by asking how Mel can possibly stay friends with a sinner like me. After all, Jesus had much to say about greed, hypocrisy, pride, and lust—sins I struggle with—but did not mention homosexuality. Even if I conclude that all homosexual behavior is wrong, as many conservative Christians do, I'm still compelled to respond with love.

> Do I believe that gay people can
> be committed Christians? Absolutely.
> I know far too many of them to doubt
> that. I also believe that alcoholics and
> prideful hypocrites can be committed
> Christians. In short, sinners can, and
> I've stepped back from ranking other
> people's sins.[30]

In an effort to reconcile his feelings with his faith, Mel believed God created him with these desires, so he embraced them. He now trusts that being a practicing homosexual and a committed Christian are compatible with his love for God. After the state of California overturned the ban on same-sex marriage, Mel married his partner of twenty-four years, Gary Nixon, on June 8, 2008. Mel has devoted himself full-time to ministering to lesbians, gays, bisexuals, and transgender people and has written extensively on the subject of gay Christians.

Two other authors who have struggled with same-sex desires and written books on the subject are Wesley Hill, *Washed and Waiting: Reflections on Christian Faithfulness and Homosexuality* and Sam Allberry, *Is God Anti-Gay?*

Both authors recognized their attraction to the same sex from an early age, both men wished desperately to have heterosexual desires, and both men recognized after all their efforts to be set free, their desires for the same sex remained the same.

However, these two authors made a different decision than Mel White to reconcile their faith to their feelings. They differentiate between the desires they were born with and acting on them. They believe it is in the acting on those desires that sin is realized. Both men love God with their whole heart and have made the lifelong decision to serve Him in their careers, but they believe the only biblical way to accomplish this is to take a vow of celibacy and not act on those desires.

While I don't understand same-sex attraction, I do understand what a tremendous sacrifice it would be for me to choose a celibate lifestyle to honor God in my life. I cannot ever question the depth of their commitment and love for God, because their sacrifice is far more than what I have ever been willing to give up: food, for example.

While I am unequivocally unqualified to explain the struggle of the person who is homosexual, I can tell you that I learned a tremendous amount from just taking the time to read the stories of these men who love God with their whole heart, and struggle with feelings of homosexuality. While homosexuality may be a choice for some, I learned by reading their stories it is clearly not a choice for all.

That realization made me feel deceived by the

Christian talking heads that I trusted, who for many years had convinced me the homosexual condition was a deliberate choice to reject their heterosexual nature and embrace a lifestyle of depravity. They spoke of and promoted successful Christian organizations offering programs to free gays and lesbians from their sinful homosexual desires through a combination of prayer and psychotherapy.

One of the first and largest of these *ex-gay* organizations was Exodus International, founded in 1976. After thirty-seven years of ministry, the board of Exodus decided to cease operations in June 2013. Then president and former homosexual Alan Chambers made the announcement that the organization no longer believed sexual orientation could be changed, even though his was. In an interview on Concordia University's campus where the announcement was made, Mr. Chambers said he believed Exodus International had helped many Christians with same-sex orientation, including himself. He then added, "Any good we could do in the future would be greatly overshadowed by the real stories of trauma and the real stories of shame. So, we decided we can't do anything but close this down."

He then issued the following apology to the LGBTQ community, which included these comments:

I am sorry for the pain and hurt that many of you have experienced. I am sorry some of you spent years working through the shame and guilt when your attractions didn't change. I am sorry we promoted sexual orientation change efforts and reparative theories about sexual orientation that stigmatized parents.

I am sorry I didn't stand up to people publicly 'on my side' who called you names like sodomite—or worse. I am sorry that I, knowing some of you so well, failed to share publicly that the gay and lesbian people I know were every bit as capable of being amazing parents as the straight people that I know. I am sorry that when I celebrated a person coming to Christ and surrendering their sexuality to Him, I callously celebrated the end of relationships that broke your heart. I am sorry I have communicated that you and your families are less than me and mine.

More than anything, I am sorry that so many have interpreted this religious rejection by Christians as God's rejection. I am profoundly sorry that many have walked away from their faith and that some have chosen to end their lives.

You have never been my enemy. I am very sorry that I have been yours.

It is strange to be someone who has both been hurt by the church's treatment of the LGBTQ community, and also to be someone who must apologize for being part of the very system of ignorance that perpetuated that hurt. Today it is as if I've just woken up to a greater sense of how painful it is to be a sinner in the hands of an angry church.[31]

An angry church? That's how the homosexual community sees us.

In Luke 10:25–37, Jesus was asked by a religious leader what he must do to inherit eternal life. Jesus then asked him to answer his own question, and the man said he should love God and love his neighbor. Jesus agreed with him, but then went on to tell a story about what a good neighbor looks like.

The Good Samaritan

Why did Jesus choose a Samaritan to be the good neighbor? Because the Samaritan people were reviled and rejected by the Jews. They were viewed as a low-class people who were the result of Jews who had intermarried with non-Jews, and they did not keep the whole of the law. But in Jesus's story, the priest and Levite—Jews who knew the law—ignored the injured man, yet the Samaritan actually followed the law by showing love to the injured man, his neighbor.

I think there are similarities between the Samaritan people of Jesus's day and the homosexual people of our day. These people and this culture are worth the effort to learn more about. Each life holds great value to our God.

We need to learn how to be good neighbors to them, and more than that, to love them. Do we want to be known as a church of hate, anger, and division, or the one that Jesus calls us to be: one of love, grace, and unity?

I don't understand the homosexual—but I don't have to. God doesn't call me to love only those people whose struggles I understand. He calls me to show grace and love to everyone, even those I don't understand.

It begins first by learning not to judge, which can be a very difficult process for many of us.

Food for Thought:

Philip Yancey shared: "Christians get very angry toward other Christians who sin differently than they do."

1. Have you witnessed this within your church community?

2. Have you experienced this in your own heart?

SEVEN

Judge Not

IN 1996 THE SUMMER Olympics were hosted by the city of Atlanta. The event was officially known as the Games of the XXVI Olympiad, but was also referred to as the Centennial Olympic Games, in celebration of the 100th anniversary of the first modern Olympic Games held in Athens in 1896. More than 10,000 athletes from 191 countries competed in Atlanta from July 19 to August 4.

In addition to the athletic competitions, there were also many organized celebrations during the seventeen days of the event. In the early morning hours of July 27, the band Jack Mack and the Heart Attack were performing in Centennial Olympic Park, which was designed to be the central gathering spot for entertainment, and showcase to the world during the Olympics.

At approximately 1:00 a.m., a thirty-three-year-old Olympic security guard noticed an unattended backpack near the sound and light tower of the concert. The security guard immediately pointed it out to the Georgia Bureau of Investigation, who then summoned the bomb squad. The security guard and other law enforcement officers worked quickly to clear the crowd, but only two to three minutes into the evacuation, several homemade pipe bombs, comprised of three-inch-long masonry nails, detonated, ultimately killing two souls and wounding 111 others.

The story of this security guard's quick discernment and action was quickly picked up by the local and national media, and he was credited with saving potentially hundreds of lives. He appeared on the *Today Show* and CNN and was interviewed by *The Atlanta Journal-Constitution*. He was congratulated by then Speaker of the House of Representatives Newt Gingrich (R-Ga.) and Senator Sam Nunn (D-Ga.).

Richard Jewell was a hero—until he wasn't.

Just three days following the bombing, information leaked from the FBI named Richard Jewell as the primary suspect in the bombing. *The Atlanta Journal-Constitution* ran the following headline on July 30, "FBI Suspects 'Hero' Guard May Have Planted Bomb"

Excerpts from the article explained the FBI's reasons for suspecting Jewell::

> The security guard who first alerted
> police to the pipe bomb that exploded

in Centennial Olympic Park is the focus of the federal investigation into the incident that resulted in two deaths and injured more than 100. Richard Jewell, 33, a former law enforcement officer, fits the profile of the lone bomber. This profile generally includes a frustrated white man who is a former police officer, member of the military or police 'wannabe' who seeks to become a hero.

In less than seventy-two hours, Richard Jewell went from hero to villain. He was immediately surrounded and hounded by the media, as his home was held under siege. On August 1, two dozen federal agents searched Jewell's apartment for over five hours, walking out with only a single box of personal items—including his mother's Tupperware. In the United States, a suspect under arrest is considered innocent until proven guilty, but for the next eighty-eight days, Richard Jewell was vilified, and his *trial* played out through all of the national mass-media outlets, with an overwhelming presumption of guilt by the public.

Richard Jewell was judged by the nation to be a villain—until he wasn't.

On October 26, almost twelve weeks after the end of the Olympics, Kent Alexander, U.S.

attorney for the Northern District of Georgia, met with one of Jewell's attorneys at a coffee shop and quietly handed him a letter stating Jewell was no longer a person of interest in the bombing investigation. But the damage was already done. Watson Bryant, Jewell's primary attorney, described the investigation this way: "This investigation was like a freight train; once it got started, it wouldn't stop."

Decades later one of the reporting journalists described the media's actions: "We in the media got it wrong, even though our reporting was right."

After the FBI acknowledged Jewell was no longer a suspect, Jewell got up in front of the media that had stalked him for so many months and marked him as notorious, and told them the following:

> This is the first time I have ever asked you to turn the cameras on me. You know my name, but you do not really know who I am. . . . For eighty-eight days I lived a nightmare. . . . I felt like a hunted animal followed constantly, waiting to be killed. . . . In their mad rush to fulfill their own personal agendas, the FBI and the media almost destroyed me and my mother. . . . The media said I was an

overzealous officer. That was a lie. I always performed my job to the best of my ability and gave 110 percent. That's not being overzealous. That's being dedicated. . . . I am going to try to re-enter law enforcement. . . . I love helping people. That's what I do, that's what I have done, and that's what I want to continue to do in the future.

I am an innocent man.

It wasn't until nine years later on April 13, 2005, that Richard Jewell was completely exonerated when Eric Rudolph, as part of a plea deal, pled guilty to the Centennial Olympic Park bombing. A little over two years later on August 29, 2007, Richard Jewell died at the young age of forty-four due to heart failure, secondary to complications of diabetes.[32,33,34, 35, 36]

Although Richard Jewell was never arrested or even charged for the Atlanta Olympic bombing, he underwent a trial by media, and the public judged him as guilty. But their judgment was wrong and destroyed the life and reputation of an innocent man.

The Bible actually has a lot to say about judging others. In John 3:17 Jesus says that God didn't send Him into the world to judge it, but to save it—even though He was unequivocally qualified to judge it.

Paul speaks about judging others in his first letter to the Corinthians. "It isn't my responsibility to judge outsiders, but it certainly is your responsibility to judge those inside the church who are sinning. God will judge those on the outside; but as the Scriptures say, 'You must remove the evil person from among you'" (1 Corinthians 5:12–13).

Paul tells the Corinthians it is the responsibility of the church to judge the sinful within its own body, and if necessary, remove them. But there is a tension between what Paul says and what Jesus says about judging others. Let's look at what Jesus tells the Jews in the Sermon on the Mount:

> Do not judge so that you will not be judged. For in the way you judge, you will be judged; and by your standard of measure, it will be measured to you. Why do you look at the speck that is in your brother's eye, but do not notice the log that is in your own eye? Or how can you say to your brother, "Let me take the speck out of your eye," and behold, the log is in your own eye? You hypocrite, first take the log out of your own eye, and then you will see clearly to take the speck out of your brother's eye. (Matthew 7:1–5 NASB)

Jesus used the term *brother* to refer to those

with sin in their lives, or with the speck in their eye, so it would certainly seem He was talking about refraining from judging someone within our own community or church. I believe Jesus's point here is this: as Christians, we are in danger of feeling self-righteous, perhaps even superior, when we accuse and condemn a brother of a sin we don't personally struggle with, yet overlook or ignore the sin in our own lives that continually causes us to stumble.

Jesus tells me not to focus on the speck of homosexuality I see in another Christian's eye when I have the log of gluttony in my own eye, making it very difficult to focus. It's a wonder I can see anything at all, as in addition to the log of gluttony, I also have:

The log of anger, which Jesus says receives the same judgment as one who has murdered.

The log of lust, which Jesus tells me is the same as committing adultery.

The log of materialism, which Paul says is the same as idolatry.

I am prone to be blinded by the log jam in my eye, yet ironically feel righteous and confident enough to point out the piece of sawdust in my brother's eye.

Perhaps the more daunting aspect of that passage is when Jesus tells me the standard by which I judge others will be the standard by which He judges me, "For in the way you judge, you will be judged; and by your standard of measure, it will be measured to you" (Matthew 7:2 NASB).

Jesus says He will look at the sin in my life with the same critical eye that I look at the sin in the homosexual person's life.

Do I really want that?

James, the brother of Jesus, said: "There will be no mercy for those who have not shown mercy to others. But if you have been merciful, God will be merciful when he judges you" (James 2:13).

For me, I have chosen to extend grace and mercy to others, including those who are homosexual, as that is the standard I want to be judged by. I need all the grace and mercy I can get.

Grace and the Law

The body of Christ has had a long-standing issue with understanding the balance between grace and sanctification. To understand grace, I think we need to first understand mercy, because grace is a giant step beyond mercy.

Mercy is not getting what I deserve. Because of the sin in my life, I deserve death, but God has shown mercy to me, and He has set me free from that death sentence. In contrast, grace is getting what I don't deserve: God's unmerited love and favor. God's grace is greater and deeper than my sin and shame, and it is something I have received apart from anything I've done.

Simply stated, there is nothing I can do to earn or deserve God's grace.

Sanctification means to "set a person apart for holiness" or "to make holy."[37] It points to righteousness or righteous living as dictated by God's law and commandments. There are some that believe sanctification is a work of the Holy Spirit alone. Others believe it is the work of the believer through the decisions and choices that are made. Still others believe it is a work of both the Holy Spirit and the believer. These two brief paragraphs do not do this complicated issue justice, but provide a glimpse of why it has been a long-standing debate in Christianity.

While I personally lean more toward the grace side of this argument, I know this is a difficult issue to wrestle with. It's easy for me to focus on the passages in the Bible that emphasize grace, but I am also very aware of the verses that emphasize right living. For example, see what Jude, the half-brother of Jesus, says about grace:

> Dear friends, I had been eagerly planning to write to you about the salvation we all share. But now I find that I must write about something else, urging you to defend the faith that God has entrusted once for all time to his holy people. I say this because some

> ungodly people have wormed their
> way into your churches, saying that
> God's marvelous grace allows us to live
> immoral lives. The condemnation of
> such people was recorded long ago, for
> they have denied our only Master and
> Lord, Jesus Christ. (Jude 3–4)

Paul wrote to the Romans about the dangers of being too comfortable with God's grace. "Well then, should we keep on sinning so that God can show us more and more of his wonderful grace? Of course not! Since we have died to sin, how can we continue to live in it?" (Romans 6:1–2)

Both authors emphasize that we should not abuse or take advantage of God's grace, and I agree wholeheartedly. And there are several passages where Paul identifies certain sins and then follows it with a statement such as, "People like this will not inherit the kingdom of God." As Christians it would be easy to assume there is a certain level of righteousness required if we are to inherit the kingdom of God and not be found guilty of abusing God's grace: that is, a lifestyle requirement to not yield to certain temptations we may be vulnerable to.

However, that assumption raises other questions like:

What is this level of righteousness we are to maintain?

How sinful do we have to be before we cross that line?

How righteous does God expect us to be to share in His kingdom?

But any of the answers to those questions would seem contrary to God's definition of grace. As Paul told the Galatians:

> Yet we know that a person is made right with God by faith in Jesus Christ, not by obeying the law. And we have believed in Christ Jesus, so that we might be made right with God because of our faith in Christ, not because we have obeyed the law. *For no one will ever be made right with God by obeying the law.*
>
> I do not treat the grace of God as meaningless. For if keeping the law could make us right with God, then there was no need for Christ to die. (Galatians 2:16, 21, emphasis added)

Hmm? This passage certainly seems to be in conflict between what Jude penned and what Paul wrote to the Romans?

Paul says no one can ever be made right with God by obeying the law. Therefore, there is no level of right living we can achieve that would ever be righteous enough. *We must rely on grace.*

In Romans Paul makes a comparison between the righteousness of the Jew and the righteousness of the Gentile—a comparison we could make between the righteousness of the heterosexual Christian and the righteousness of the homosexual Christian:

> Well then, should we conclude that we Jews are better than others *[heterosexual Christians are better than homosexual Christians]*? No, not at all, for we have already shown that all people, whether Jews or Gentiles *[heterosexual or homosexual]*, are under the power of sin. As the Scriptures say, "No one is righteous—not even one. No one is truly wise; no one is seeking God. All have turned away; all have become useless. No one does good, not a single one. Their talk is foul, like the stench from an open grave. Their tongues are filled with lies. Snake venom drips from their lips. Their mouths are full of cursing and bitterness. They rush to commit murder. Destruction and misery always follow them. They don't know where to find peace. They have no fear of God at all." Obviously, the law applies to those to whom it was given, for its purpose is to keep people

from having excuses, and to show that
the entire world is guilty before God.
For no one can ever be made right with
God by doing what the law commands.
The law simply shows us how sinful
we are. (Romans 3:9–20, emphasis
added)

There it is again: we can never be made right
with God through our own righteousness. The law
is there to remind us of how sinful we *all* are. If
those who act on their homosexual temptations
are committing sin, then those who act on their
gluttony, lust, and materialism are also committing
sin. With that said, wouldn't it seem that the
church should treat homosexuality—a sin many
Christians aren't tempted by—in the same way it
treats the sins (logs) that many Christians struggle
with and are more sympathetic toward?

Paul's Personal Letter to Timothy

Paul is generally credited with being the
author of thirteen books of the New Testament.
Of those thirteen books, or letters, ten of them
were written to and meant to be shared with the
churches he founded and/or visited. Three of them,
however, were personal letters, commonly referred
to as pastoral letters. These were letters written near

the end of his life to fellow pastors and friends, giving advice and instruction on dealing with the challenges of running a church community. These letters were perhaps never intended to be shared with the church body outside of leadership.

Yet they were, and, as a result, we gain insight into Paul's shortcomings as he shares of his humanity and struggles. Two of those three letters were written to Timothy, whom he referred to as his "true son in the faith." In the first chapter of his first letter to Timothy, almost in his opening remarks, he told Timothy this:

> This is a trustworthy saying, and everyone should accept it: "Christ Jesus came into the world to save sinners"—and I am the worst of them all. But God had mercy on me so that Christ Jesus could use me as a prime example of his great patience with even the worst sinners. Then others will realize that they, too, can believe in him and receive eternal life. (1 Timothy 1:15–16)

Though Paul was a teacher and mentor to Timothy, he admitted to his student that he was the worst of all sinners. For years, I interpreted that to refer to the time before Paul met Christ on the road to Damascus—a time when he, in his ignorance,

persecuted Christ's church to the extent of organiz-
ing the killing of those in the Christian faith. Paul
references that time in his life in the three verses
prior. But Paul doesn't say he *was* the worst of all
sinners; he said he *is* the worst of them all. Was he
saying he is the worst sinner of them all because of
what he did or because of what he was still doing?

I don't know why it was difficult for me to accept
sin was an issue in Paul's life. I guess I assumed since
he was responsible for writing so much of the New
Testament, and he personally met Jesus after His
ascension from this earth, that he had risen above
his chains of humanity and the temptations of this
world. But John reminds us, "If we claim we have
no sin, we are only fooling ourselves and not living
in the truth" (1 John 1:8).

If we are human, we sin. Paul was human;
therefore, he struggled with sin just like we do. Paul
even warned the Galatians of this continual inner
battle for the Christian. "The sinful nature wants
to do evil, which is just the opposite of what the
Spirit wants. And the Spirit gives us desires that
are the opposite of what the sinful nature desires.
These two forces are constantly fighting each other, so
you are not free to carry out your good intentions"
(Galatians 5:17, emphasis added).

Just like us, Paul had a constant battle taking
place inside of him between his flesh and the Spirit.

Sometimes he won the battle, but I'm sure he lost sometimes and gave in to temptation. In Paul's mind, he believed himself to be the worst sinner of them all.

Thorn in the Flesh

In Paul's second letter to the Corinthians, he refers to a *thorn in his flesh*. "So to keep me from becoming proud, I was given a thorn in my flesh, a messenger from Satan to torment me and keep me from becoming proud. Three different times I begged the Lord to take it away. Each time he said, 'My grace is all you need. My power works best in weakness'" (2 Corinthians 12:7–9).

What was Paul's thorn in the flesh?

Nobody knows.

We do know Paul was not talking about a literal thorn. It is understood that he was speaking metaphorically. One prominent theory is that he was speaking of a physical ailment. He refers to being sick in his letter to the Galatians:

> Surely you remember that I was sick when I first brought you the Good News. But even though my condition tempted you to reject me, you did not despise me or turn me away. No, you took me in and cared for me

as though I were an angel from God or even Christ Jesus himself. Where is that joyful and grateful spirit you felt then? I am sure you would have taken out your own eyes and given them to me if it had been possible. (Galatians 4:13–15)

Some believe he had a disease in his eye, which would explain why he told the Galatians at the end of his letter, "Notice what large letters I use as I write these closing words in my own handwriting" (Galatians 6:11), the argument being he was writing large letters so he could see what he was writing.

Others believe his thorn was a reference to the Jewish community or to an individual who continued to harass and persecute him. In Paul's second letter to Timothy, he referenced Alexander the coppersmith who "did me much harm" (2 Timothy 4:14–15).

However, another less popular theory is that Paul was referring to a carnal temptation he never achieved control over. We typically dismiss this idea quickly because we tend to put Paul on a spiritual pedestal and believe him to be above any worldly temptations. But Paul told Timothy he was the worst of all sinners. He also refers to his thorn in the flesh as "a messenger from Satan." While the

Bible tells us that not all temptation comes from Satan (James 1:13–14), it also illustrates that enticement can come from the devil. Peter accused Ananias of temptation from the devil. "Why have you let Satan fill your heart? You lied to the Holy Spirit, and you kept some of the money for yourself" (Acts 5:3).

Luke 22:3 and John 13:2 make it pretty clear Satan was responsible for tempting Judas to betray Jesus, and it was Satan tempting Jesus when He was in the wilderness. God's answer to Paul's pleading to be released from his thorn in the flesh was, "My grace is all you need." Certainly, grace is the answer we all seek when we confess our sin to Christ.

Could it be Paul struggled with a temptation he would sometimes yield to? Was the struggle he battled and referred to as "common to man" (1 Corinthians 10:13), carnal enticement? Was the temptation there to keep him from becoming spiritually proud and having a sense of superiority, as the Pharisees did?

While no one knows for sure what Paul was talking about when he referenced his thorn in the flesh, it is probably a good thing it was intentionally referred to in such a vague way so it could be applied to our various struggles, whether physical, emotional, or spiritual.

The Righteousness of the Christian

How does God see our best effort at right living? Isaiah describes it this way: "We are all infected and impure with sin. When we display our righteous deeds, they are nothing but filthy rags" (Isaiah 64:6).

Matthew Poole's Commentary defines a *filthy rag* as "a cloth made up of patches, or such as come from a putrid sore, or defiled with the menstruous blood of a woman."[38] To the Jews, this metaphor used to describe their righteousness could be summed up in one word—disgusting.

God saved you by his grace when you believed. And you can't take credit for this; it is a gift from God. Salvation is not a reward for the good things we have done, so none of us can boast about it (Ephesians 2:8–9).

Salvation is free, so we have to be cautious about not trying to earn it. Good works are not a requirement of salvation; they are a result of it. None of us is righteous. None of us has achieved a level of righteousness that impresses God or negates the need for His mercy and grace and the death of Jesus on the cross to reconcile us to Him.

None of us.

Without even trying, the general public judged Richard Jewell guilty in his media trial. I think it was human nature. As Christians, that same tendency to judge those who are different from us is part of our human nature as well. It's easy to fall into that trap, so we need to remind ourselves that to God we are all on an even playing field. He sees all of our sin and still chooses to extend us His grace. But unless we want God to judge us by the same standard we use to judge the person who is homosexual—as He warned us He would do—I would encourage you to "judge not."

Food for Thought:

Comparison plays an integral role in judging others. I often look at my life and my sins and make a comparison to what I see in others. Before I can feel justified in judging someone else, I need to draw the conclusion that my sins are not as bad as another's, so I can feel confidant—or at least comfortable—to pass judgment.

1. Have you witnessed this within your church community?
2. Have you experienced this in your own heart?

EIGHT

Is Jesus Christ the Same Yesterday, Today, and Forever?

I WAS ALWAYS TAUGHT that God never changes, with the foundation for this teaching clearly outlined in the Bible. Moses said, "God is not a man, so he does not lie. He is not human, so he does not change his mind" (Numbers 23:19).

James also speaks of His unchanging nature. "He never changes or casts a shifting shadow" (James 1:17). The psalmist praised God for His unchanging character: "But you [God] are always the same; you will live forever" (Psalm 102:27).

And God Himself declared through His prophet Malachi, "I am the Lord, and I do not change." (Malachi 3:6)

And there are many more.

So, since God is the same yesterday, today, and forever (Hebrews 13:8), then we can assume His attitude toward people who are homosexual hasn't changed either. As Christians we argue that the principles outlined in Scripture are continually under attack by an increasingly liberal, North

American culture. However, if we read the Bible with integrity and are honest, our present-day Christian culture is guilty of the same and has allowed a not so subtle erosion of some of His laws and decrees as well. Here are some examples:

God first tells the Israelites in Leviticus 19:19, "You must obey all my decrees."

Then He continues on in the same verse and says, "Do not wear clothing woven from two different kinds of thread."

Guilty.

You could consider this a lifestyle sin for me. If you were to peruse my closet, you would be hard-pressed to find any item of clothing that wasn't a blend of some type. Let's be honest, I don't know anyone who would even consider this a sin.

But wait—there's more: Leviticus 19:27 says, "Do not trim off the hair on your temples or trim your beards."

Guilty again.

It's difficult to find hard facts on this subject, but in an online search, I found that 43–67 percent of men are clean shaven and would be in violation of this decree. (I didn't even try and search for men who trim the hair on their temples). I have a beard, but I keep it closely trimmed, also a clear violation of this law.

In the very next verse, 28, we find: "…do not mark your skin with tattoos. I am the Lord."

There is an ever-increasing shift in our culture toward the acceptance of tattoos, for both men and women. While I do not have a tattoo, all four of my children have at least one, and I am not the least bit concerned about their eternal destiny. Why?

I mean if God doesn't change, why is it that when we read these declarations from God, we dismiss them? Could it be we see no real, moral foundation for these decrees and certainly no present-day application for them? If this is true, why did God record them? Let's take a closer look at some of the beliefs and practices surrounding Christianity today.

Present-Day Christian Culture

Today finding clothing made from one type of thread would be the exception rather than the norm, so most of us ignore that passage. When was the last time you knelt down and asked God to forgive you because you wore a cotton/poly-blend shirt all day?

Today we view a clean-shaven man as clean-cut and therefore as wholesome, respectful, reverent— exactly the image Les Schwab Tire Centers wants to convey by being closed on Sundays and requiring all their employees to have no facial hair. Yet this employment requirement stands in stark contrast to God's actual decree concerning facial hair. Can you even imagine a pastor confronting his clean-shaven congregation for violating this law of God?

Today I know several pastors who have tattoos. They often choose to mark themselves with biblical verses, spiritual sayings, or drawings, with the goal being to initiate a discussion about Jesus with an unsaved person. Surely there can't be anything wrong with a tattoo if it is used as a tool for evangelism, right?

Like the sin of gluttony, the twenty-first century, North American Christian culture has white-washed all of these inconvenient—and what we believe are inconsequential—sins. Yet these presumed inconsequential sins are found in the same chapter as these commands that are more widely accepted and haven't changed with time:

> Each of you must show great respect for your mother and father, and you must always observe my Sabbath days of rest. I am the Lord your God. (Leviticus 19:3)

> Do not put your trust in idols or make metal images of gods for yourselves. I am the Lord your God. (Leviticus 19:4)

> Do not steal. Do not deceive or cheat one another. (Leviticus 19:11)

> Do not bring shame on the name of your God by using it to swear falsely. I am the Lord. (Leviticus 19:12)

> Do not defraud or rob your neighbor. (Leviticus 19:13)

> Love your neighbor as yourself. I am the Lord. (Leviticus 19:18)

In the very same chapter of the Bible where we've chosen to ignore several of God's seemingly inconsequential commands, we also read the requirements of the Ten Commandments, with the last one being quoted by Jesus in the New Testament as one of the greatest commandments. The church typically doesn't ignore or gloss over the commands to not steal or cheat or have idols, or the command to love your neighbor. I mean those are part of the Ten Commandments, and we'd never contradict one of the big ten, would we?

Unfortunately, even the Ten Commandments aren't sacred to our present-day Christian culture, as many of us disregard His fourth commandment on a regular basis: "Remember the Sabbath day and keep it holy." Often the god of recreation wins out instead. Whether knowingly or unknowingly, we all pick and choose which of His laws we think He is serious about, especially if they interfere with what we want to do. We might think to ourselves: *I want to have a tattoo to make a lifelong statement or to reach the lost or because it's pretty. I want to keep my beard and temple hair trimmed so I don't look like the guys from Duck Dynasty. I want to wear clothes made from two threads, so I can look my best for God.*

As we read many of the instructions God gave the Jewish nation of the Old Testament, we interpret them through the lens of our present-day culture and then dismiss them as outdated or irrelevant. This isn't God changing His mind, but our Christian culture changing our attitudes toward those commands. However, there are several passages in the Bible where it sure seems like God changed His mind. Here's a tough one. "Anyone who dishonors [Anyone who speaks disrespectfully of] father or mother must be put to death. Such a person is guilty of a capital offense" (Leviticus 20:9).

Then Moses expounds on this law in detail again in Deuteronomy:

> Suppose a man has a stubborn and
> rebellious son who will not obey his

father or mother, even though they
discipline him. In such a case, the
father and mother must take the son
to the elders as they hold court at the
town gate. The parents must say to the
elders, 'This son of ours is stubborn
and rebellious and refuses to obey. He
is a glutton and a drunkard.' Then all
the men of his town must stone him
to death. In this way, you will purge
this evil from among you, and all
Israel will hear about it and be afraid.
(Deuteronomy 21:18–21)

I'm thinking the population of the North
American church would be much smaller today if
we followed that command. Even though Leviticus
and Deuteronomy record these instructions from
God to put to death those who are rebellious and
disrespectful toward their parents, I don't believe
He wants us to obey this command today, no
matter how insolent our children might be. There
is no reference in the Bible documenting the Jews
acting on this commandment, but there are stories
about prodigal children coming back to a right
relationship with their families and God. Does that
mean He has changed His mind on parenting and
childhood discipline?

Here's another one regarding something I

believe God finds detestable today. He gave the following instructions:

> However, you may purchase male and female slaves from among the nations around you. You may also purchase the children of temporary residents who live among you, including those who have been born in your land. You may treat them as your property, passing them on to your children as a permanent inheritance. You may treat them as slaves, but you must never treat your fellow Israelites this way. (Leviticus 25:44–46)

Treating people as property flies in the face of so many other teachings evidenced throughout Scripture regarding the sanctity of human life, liberty, and freedom proclaimed for all of God's people.

Does that mean He changed His mind toward slavery?

This next example seems to clearly document God changing His mind. In Leviticus 11, God gave detailed instructions to Moses and Aaron regarding which animals were considered ceremonially clean and therefore okay to eat, and which animals were unclean and should not to be eaten. This is a very lengthy passage on dietary requirements, so I'm not going to quote it here, but I encourage you to read it on your own if you are having trouble sleeping. However, I do want to point out that bacon was included on that list of unclean and forbidden foods. Can you imagine life without bacon?

We read in the New Testament twice about how God gave instructions contradicting what he told Moses and Aaron. First in His vision to Peter:

> He [Peter] saw the sky open, and something like a large sheet was let down by its four corners. In the sheet were all sorts of animals, reptiles, and birds. Then a voice said to him, "Get up, Peter; kill and eat them." "No, Lord," Peter declared. "I have never eaten anything that our Jewish laws have declared impure and unclean." But the voice spoke again: "Do not call something unclean if God has made it clean." The same vision was repeated three times. Then the sheet was suddenly pulled up to heaven. (Acts 10:11–16)

We read of this again when Jesus was explaining a parable to His disciples:

"Don't you understand either?" he asked. "Can't you see that the food you put into your body cannot defile you? Food doesn't go into your heart, but only passes through the stomach and then goes into the sewer." [By saying this, he declared that every kind of food is acceptable in God's eyes.] (Mark 7:18–19)

At face value, it seems God did change His mind regarding dietary restrictions. Under Old Testament law, God clearly stated certain foods were not to be eaten, and then in the New Testament those same foods are declared clean and okay to eat. However, I'm not convinced these are examples of God changing His mind. Let me explain.

After Jesus had been tempted in the desert, right at the beginning of His ministry, He returned to His hometown and went to the synagogue. He was handed the scroll of Isaiah, and He turned to chapter 61 and read the first two verses aloud.

"When he came to the village of Nazareth, his boyhood home, he went as usual to the synagogue on the Sabbath and stood up to read the Scriptures. The scroll of Isaiah the prophet was handed to him. He unrolled the scroll and found the place where this was written:

"The Spirit of the LORD is upon me,
for he has anointed me to bring Good
News to the poor. He has sent me to
proclaim that captives will be released,
that the blind will see, that the oppressed will be set free, and that the
time of the LORD's favor has come."
(Luke 4:16–19)

Let's stop for a minute to understand what Isaiah was referring to when they declared the arrival
of "the time of the Lord's favor." It's a reference to
the year of Jubilee described in Leviticus 25. Every
fiftieth year was proclaimed the year of Jubilee for
the Israelites, and it was made up of three required
features:

1. *The practice of letting their land lie fallow.* Leaving their land unplanted enabled it to rest and
   become replenished and fertile. It also meant
   there was much less work to be done since they
   weren't having to tend to a crop or harvest one,
   allowing the workers to rest as well.
2. *The compulsory return of all property to its original owners or heirs.* All land that had been sold
   during the previous forty-nine years was then
   required to be returned to the original family
   owners. This would reestablish the original di-

vision of properties when God gave them the land.

3. *A proclamation of freedom to all slaves.* This included indentured servants who, compelled by poverty, had sold themselves as slaves to their brothers to support their families. All regained their liberty and cancelation of debt in the year of Jubilee.

These three requirements for the year of Jubilee referenced in Isaiah 61:1–2 would have been well understood by Jesus's Jewish audience in the temple where He was reading. However, Jesus communicated a fourth aspect when He intentionally didn't read the last sentence of this passage. If you read Isaiah 61:2 in its entirety it says, "He has sent me to tell those who mourn that the time of the Lord's favor has come, and with it, the day of God's anger against their enemies."

Jesus deliberately left off the part about God's anger and judgment being exercised against the enemies of Israel, which was always thought to be included in the year of Jubilee. No doubt when Jesus stopped reading, the other men listening must have been waiting for Him to finish the passage. Luke tells us what happened: "He rolled up the scroll, handed it back to the attendant, and sat down. All eyes in the synagogue looked at him intently. Then he began to speak to them. 'The Scripture you've just heard has been fulfilled this very day!'" (Luke 4:20–21)

Instead of reading the last phrase of the passage, Jesus stopped short and told His Jewish audience the Scripture He read from was fulfilled this day—through Him. The problem was, it wasn't the year of Jubilee. According to calculations by theologians much smarter than me, AD 6 was the last year of Jubilee (when Jesus would have been a young child), and the next year of Jubilee wasn't until AD 55 (long after Jesus's death.[39]). So why was Jesus proclaiming this time in history as the year of Jubilee when it clearly wasn't? I believe He was declaring, at the beginning of His ministry, that His presence in humanity as the Messiah was ushering in the *age* of Jubilee. An age about God showing His favor rather than His vengeance or judgment. An age that would not end until Jesus's return at the second coming.

The age of grace.

Jesus was asked by John the Baptist's disciples if He was the Messiah. "Jesus told them, "Go back to John and tell him what you have heard and seen—the blind see, the lame walk, those with leprosy are cured, the deaf hear, the dead are raised to life, and the Good News is being preached to the poor" (Matthew 11:4–5).

The good news Jesus announced wasn't about God's judgment and condemnation; they had already been living under that for millennia. No, the good news was an announcement of something new—a new covenant. The good news was about His undeserved and unfailing love. This *age* of Jubilee was no longer about following the rules and regulations of the law, but instead, about a personal relationship with Jesus Christ.

John provides a clear understanding of why Jesus came to earth. "God sent his Son into the world not to judge the world, but to save the world through him" (John 3:17).

This good news was always a part of God's game plan. God shared it through His prophet Isaiah almost seven hundred years before the birth of Jesus. God didn't change His mind; it was always His plan that Jesus would become the Savior for mankind. Jesus ushering in the age of Jubilee was God's plan from the beginning of time—a new age that is all about the law of love and not the law of Moses.

Homosexuality and Culture

Is homosexuality a cultural issue?

With its growing acceptance in North American, secular culture, the answer would be yes. However, despite the church's cultural acceptance of closely shaved men, trimmed hair, poly-blended clothes, and tattoos—homosexuality within the North American, Christian culture is flatly rejected and considered unacceptable and morally depraved. It seems to me the church is again applying a double standard.

What does the age of Jubilee toward the homosexual look like in the twenty-first century?

That's what we'll look at in the next chapter.

Food for thought:

Tattoos, haircuts, and poly-blend clothes—I don't know anyone who would consider these decrees from God as sin. All of us ignore them and give them no credence. And the seriousness of keeping the Sabbath continues to falter.

1. Why can we definitely dismiss these decrees and yet know God is still serious about His commandments to not steal, lie, cheat, or have other gods before you and to honor your mother and father?

2. Are there other decrees God gives in the Old Testament that may no longer be consequential?

NINE

What Does Fair Look Like?

I READILY ADMIT I am unqualified to write this book, with the exception that I would put my skills as a glutton up against any man (or woman). For the last forty years, I have worked in the medical field—first as a paramedic, then a registered nurse, and, for the last twenty-eight years, as a clinical perfusionist: that's the person running the heart-lung machine during open-heart surgery. I have no formal biblical training, but I have been a follower of Christ for all of my adult life and am devoted to His Word; I read and study the Bible almost daily, and I listen to His teachers almost weekly.

I made a deal with God several years ago regarding the writing of this book, similar to what Gideon did in chapter 6 of Judges. God came through on His end of the deal, but I kept trying to remind Him how unqualified I was to take on this sort of issue, so I dodged Him for two more years until I reluctantly began the process.

I know how controversial this subject is, so I want to address something I was concerned of being accused of: I don't want to be the false teacher the Bible warns Christians about. In Ephesians 4:14, Paul encourages the people of Ephesus and explains why they need to grow and mature in the Lord. "Then we will no longer be immature like children. We won't be tossed and blown about by every wind of new teaching. We will not be influenced when people try to trick us with lies so clever they sound like the truth."

Peter also warns the churches of Asia Minor against false prophets.

> But there were also false prophets in Israel, just as there will be false teachers among you. They will cleverly teach destructive heresies and even deny the Master who bought them. In this way, they will bring sudden destruction on themselves. Many will follow their evil teaching and shameful immorality. And because of these teachers, the way of truth will be slandered. In their greed they will make up clever lies to get hold of your money. But God condemned them long ago, and their destruction will not be delayed. (2 Peter 2:1–3)

So, let me say clearly again: homosexuality is a sin—but so is gluttony, pride, materialism, gossiping, having a critical spirit, and so forth. I didn't write this book to excuse the sin of homosexuality, but rather to point out how the church treats that lifestyle sin differently than the other lifestyle sins Christians wrestle with. As someone who takes fairness very seriously, I believe the church should be fair and consistent in how people are treated.

The purpose of this book is not to provide the answers, but to ask the questions that will get the church to engage in the discussion. This subject has been off-limits within the church community for far too long. The few gutsy pastors who have risked their reputations and credibility by addressing this topic from a different or contrary viewpoint should be recognized as courageous. Let me ask two questions for us to think about to further this discussion:

Can a practicing homosexual be a Christian?

If the answer to that question is *no*, then the next question should be:

Can a practicing glutton be a Christian?

If we are being fair, then the answer should be the same.

However, if we do believe practicing homosexuals can be Christians, then we need to change our attitudes and actions toward them. The church should be a place that welcomes the LGBTQ community to live out their faith and express their love for God through serving and loving others—just as it does for the rest of us.

So, what does the church being fair look like? I believe it should contain at least three actions: treating people with consistency, reading the Bible with integrity, and modeling the life of Christ. I'll address the first two actions here and the third action in chapter 11.

Consistency

It is shameful to me how quickly we as a church brand homosexuals as immoral and undeserving of a relationship with Christ, while we not only tolerate, but sometimes celebrate, the sins that the majority of the church body struggles with, *and yields to*, on a weekly basis.

Whatever limitations your church community feels are biblically appropriate for the homosexual should also be applied to the glutton, the proud, the materialistic, the gossip, the critical spirit, and so forth.

If practicing homosexuals are not allowed to become members of the church, then neither should practicing gluttons. If gays and lesbians aren't allowed positions of leadership, then neither should the materialistic.

Reading with Integrity

I believe the Bible should be the foundation for setting the standard by which the local church addresses this issue, but let's use integrity when using the Bible to define our position. In other words, don't pick and choose snippets of isolated Scripture that support our feelings.

Paul addressed sinful desires in his letter to the Galatians. "When you follow the desires of your sinful nature, the results are very clear: sexual immorality, impurity, lustful pleasures. Let me tell you again, as I have before, that anyone living that sort of life will not inherit the Kingdom of God" (Galatians 5:19, 21).

It would be easy to say, "Well, homosexuality clearly falls under the definition of sexual immorality and lustful pleasure, and Paul made it clear they will not inherit the kingdom of God, so they are going to hell."

But that is not reading the Bible with integrity.

You see viewing pornography would also fall under the same categories of sexual immorality and lustful pleasure. As I mentioned before, 50 percent of surveyed pastors admitted to viewing pornography in the last year, so I think it's safe to say at least 50 percent of the men in your church have probably yielded to the same temptation. Using the same standard we just applied to homosexuals, that means at least 50 percent of the men in your church—members, leaders, deacons, elders, pastors—would also not inherit the kingdom of God and they would also be going to hell.

What's more, we need to look at the entire paragraph Paul wrote, including verse 20 and the rest of verse 21:

> When you follow the desires of your sinful nature, the results are very clear: sexual immorality, impurity, lustful pleasures, idolatry, sorcery, hostility, quarreling, jealousy, outbursts of anger, selfish ambition, dissension, division, envy, drunkenness, wild parties, *and other sins like these*. Let me tell you again, as I have before, that anyone living that sort of life will not inherit the Kingdom of God. (Galatians 5:19–21, emphasis added)

Isn't it interesting how Paul included what we might consider to be minor sins—hostility, quarreling, jealousy, outbursts of anger, selfish ambition, dissension, and envy—with what we would consider to be the more serious sins of sexual immorality, impurity, lustful pleasures, idolatry, division, and sorcery? Then he said clearly that anyone who lives a life that includes *any* of these sins will not inherit the kingdom of God.

Can that really be true?

If it is, can anyone inherit the kingdom of God? I don't know many Christians who don't "follow the desires of their sinful nature" in at least one of those listed areas, or in the catch-all category of "other sins like these."

Are we all going to hell? Is that what Jesus meant with his teaching in the Sermon on the Mount?

"'For the gate is wide and the way is easy that leads to destruction, and those who enter by it are many. For the gate is narrow and the way is hard that leads to life, and those who find it are few'" (Matthew 7:13–14 ESV).

Who in the world can be saved? Jesus's answer to that very question was, "'Humanly speaking, it is impossible. But with God everything is possible'" (Matthew 19:26).

This is the kind of discussion the church should wrestle with in its search for the truth and God's heart toward the homosexual community, or any issue for that matter. As the church, we are the bride of Christ, His representative on this earth. We need to be careful to represent His heart and attitude toward any matter. We need to read His Word with *integrity* and apply it *consistently*.

The Stakes Are Higher Than We Know

This battle is not just about the hearts and minds of the homosexual community—it is much bigger than that. In 2015, CNN reported on a landmark study conducted by the Pew Research Center which documents, "Millennials are leaving the church in droves!"[40]

Another study by the Public Religion Research Institute in 2016 reported the number of Americans between the ages of eighteen and twenty-nine who identify themselves as having *no religious affiliation* has nearly quadrupled in the last thirty years.[41]

In 2011, a Barna study reported there wasn't just one isolated reason for the mass exodus of millennials from the faith, but there was one consistent issue in the forefront of this research: *the perception of judgmental attitudes around sex and sexuality.*[42]

Here are some more telling statistics about the gravity of this issue:

- Nearly seven in ten (69%) millennials agree that religious groups are alienating young people by being too judgmental about gay and lesbian issues. A majority (56%) of Americans age thirty to forty-nine also agree.[43]
- More than six in ten Americans believe the messages about homosexuality coming from

America's places of worship contribute either a lot (23%) or a little (40%) to higher rates of suicide among gay and lesbian youth.[44]

- Millennials felt churches should focus their engagement on actions that serve the common good or should speak up for the oppressed, rather than opposing a controversial issue because of theological objections.[45]

Let me try and clarify the importance of these sobering statistics. My age puts me near the end of the baby-boom generation. Growing up, and for most of my adult life, I referred to gays and lesbians as, "*Those people.*"

The millennial generation refers to them as, "*My friend.*"

This is an example of the kind of inconsistency they struggle with. They have a hard time reconciling the presumed message from the church that there is an all-loving God who wants a relationship with them, but who rejects the marginalized gay community—their friends. They require of us a transparent and unapologetic honesty regarding issues of faith and religion, and they are looking for consistency and integrity in their practical application. They are looking for consistency in how and whom the church loves, and integrity in how the church interprets and applies scriptural truth.

If we as the church don't get this issue right, we risk not only alienating a segment of society, but also losing an entire *generation*.

This young generation is willing to not only look at, but also examine the passages of Scripture we as the church have often chosen to ignore. The answer, "This is what we've always believed," is no longer an adequate explanation from the church. We need to dig deeper and recognize this is a multidimensional issue, and not base our attitudes and actions toward the LGBTQ community on a few verses that we don't have the integrity to embrace in their entirety.

This is what is at stake with the decisions we make today. How would Jesus feel if we took the easy way out and just kept thinking and doing things the way we've always thought and done them?

We'll look at that in the next chapter.

Food for Thought

Herd mentality, also known as mob mentality, describes how people can be influenced by their peers to adopt certain behaviors on a largely emotional, rather than rational, basis. When individuals are affected by mob mentality, they may make different decisions than they would have individually.[46] No one wants to admit their actions may be explained away by being part of the crowd, and I believe they often hope they would have the courage to go against the crowd when it's appropriate. But...

1. Have your attitudes and actions toward the LGBTQ community been influenced by what others in your faith community believe?
2. At the risk of not only losing a segment of society that is different, but also an entire generation, could you display the courage required to walk against the herd if you believed that is what Scripture revealed?

TEN

What Makes Jesus Mad?

ONE OF THE GREAT mysteries of the Christian faith is the doctrine of incarnation: Jesus was fully God and fully man. Deity and humanity. And while we may have a hard time explaining it, we certainly enjoy celebrating it at Christmas. The fact that Jesus was human means He shared human emotions. He expressed agape love and received philia love throughout His life on earth. He experienced sadness as He was moved to tears when He witnessed Lazarus's sisters' sense of loss in John 11:35. The New Testament writers also let us know that He experienced anger.

If we examine the life of Christ here on earth, we can see who or what it was that made Jesus angry.

I would place the demons that Jesus rebuked for their oppression and cruelty of God's children (see partial list in Luke 4 and Mark 1) at the top of the list for making Jesus angry.

Then running a close second would be the religious leaders of His day. Luke 11, Matthew 23, and Mark 3 clearly record Jesus's expression of anger toward their holier-than-thou hypocrisy.

Next on my list, I would put the money changers and those selling the animals used for sacrifice in the Jewish temple. All four Gospels record this event and show Jesus's anger toward those opportunists exploiting and profiting from the required Jewish Passover, and using the temple to do so (Matthew 21, Mark 11, Luke 19, and John 2).

Also, I would include the disciples. And while it certainly seems like there were times He was angry with them, I would like to think it was more out of frustration because I've done some pretty boneheaded things like they did (Matthew 16, Mark 8, Luke 9).

Last but not least, a fig tree (Mark 11).

What's interesting is if you look at everyone and everything Jesus was angry with, it wasn't the notorious sinners of His day like you might expect. Yet we as Christ's representatives have chosen to express His anger toward homosexuals, this small subset of sinners.

If Jesus didn't express His anger toward the sinners of His day, why do we assume it is our responsibility as His bride to convey His anger to this select group of sinners in our day? Is this the attitude that will lead the lost toward a relationship with Christ? The Bible describes just the opposite.

Responding with Kindness

Paul wrote to the church in Rome expressing what it takes to draw someone into a right relationship with God. "Or do you think lightly of the riches of His kindness and tolerance and patience, not knowing that the kindness of God leads you to repentance?" (Romans 2:4 NASB)

Paul encourages us to not overlook or diminish the depth of God's patience and *tolerance* toward the unsaved. He proclaims that it is God's kindness that leads us to repentance and a changed life, not the judgment of God.

At two different times John records Jesus as saying, "I did not come to judge (condemn) the world, but to save it" (John 3:17, John 12:47). Jesus lived out what Paul told the church in Rome by showing the unsaved of His day the kindness of God—not His judgment.

Jesus never intended His presence with sinners to be interpreted as condoning their sin, nor did He participate in it. Jesus's presence among sinners revealed the kindness of God that could lead them to a changed life through repentance.

It is this same kindness we as Christians rely on as we continue in the lifestyle sins of gluttony, materialism, and pride to hopefully and eventually bring about in us this changed life. There is grace in this life, and we aren't expected to be perfect in all things. Look at what Paul told the Philippians about his own shortcomings, "I don't mean to say that I have already achieved these things or that I have already reached perfection. But I press on to possess that perfection for which Christ Jesus first possessed me. No, dear brothers and sisters, I have not achieved it" (Philippians 3:12–13).

Paul admitted he hadn't achieved the perfect walk with God, and neither have we; we are all relying on God's grace. So, shouldn't we as the body of Christ, extend this same godly, "kindness, tolerance, and patience" toward all sinners, including gays and lesbians, by showing the mercy, love, and compassion Jesus showed to all those around Him?

Many of us have friends or family, people whom we love, who aren't saved. Do you realize in God's eyes they are in the same category as any person who is not a follower of Christ? This includes the unbelieving homosexual, pedophile, and terrorist. They are unsaved and are committing the unforgivable sin of denying Jesus Christ and rejecting His love and ultimate sacrifice on the cross. Homosexuality itself isn't the unforgivable sin, yet the church seems to treat homosexuals as if they are unforgivable.

Which church culture do you believe your unsaved loved one would be more likely to respond to—the judgmental climate many churches have created toward the LGBTQ community, or one that exemplifies the kindness, mercy, and compassion of God?

The answer is obvious, isn't it?

The Twenty-First Century Church and the Issue of Pride

No Christian book would be complete without a quote from C.S. Lewis, so let me include this one. "According to Christian teachers, the essential vice, the utmost evil, is Pride. Unchastity, anger, greed, drunkenness, and all that, are mere flea bites in comparison: it was through Pride that the devil became the devil: Pride leads to every other vice: it is the complete anti-God state of mind.[47]"

The sin of the Pharisees was their hard-heartedness, hypocrisy, and religious *pride*. They thought they were morally and spiritually superior—Jesus didn't have a very high opinion of them. Could the twenty-first-century church be guilty of the same thing?

On March 24, 2014, Richard Stearns, then president of World Vision USA, made an announcement through an interview with *Christianity Today* about the organization's decision to hire gay Christians in same-sex marriages:

"Changing the employee conduct policy to allow someone in a same-sex marriage who is a professed believer in Jesus Christ to work for us makes our policy more consistent with our practice on other divisive issues. It also allows us to treat all of our employees the same way: abstinence outside of marriage, and fidelity within marriage.[48]"

In reading this, it would be easy to assume World Vision's endorsement of the homosexual agenda, but this was far from it. In the same interview, he expanded on the organization's motivation for the change:

It's easy to read a lot more into this decision than is really there. This is not an endorsement of same-sex marriage. We have decided we are not going to get into that debate. Nor is this a rejection of traditional marriage, which we affirm and support.

We're not caving to some kind of pressure. We're not on some slippery slope. There is no lawsuit threatening us. There is no employee group lobbying us. This is not us compromising. It is us deferring to the authority of churches and denominations on theological issues. We're an operational arm of the global church, we're not a theological arm of the church. This is simply a decision about whether or not you are eligible for employment at World Vision US based on this single issue, and nothing more.

Seems innocent enough. However, the *Huffington Post* reported on the effect of this announcement in a December 2014 article: "Two days later, under immense financial pressure and criticism from gatekeepers on the evangelical right, World Vision USA reversed their decision, breaking hearts, promises, and leaving an utter leadership vacuum on one of the church's most divisive issues."[49]

Then there was this staggering fallout about their transitory, two-day long decision: "After announcing the decision, World Vision lost between 3,000 and 3,500 sponsors for needy children across the globe as evangelical groups across the country called for a boycott."[50]

Let's try and wrap our heads around this. More than three thousand people, a number that doesn't even include all of those who threatened World Vision if they didn't change their decision, walked away from their commitment to an innocent child—a child struggling to survive on a monthly donation that would provide only the basics of subsistence. What did these children have to do with World Vision's decision to change their hiring practices?

Did these same people who were offended by World Vision's decision to hire Christians in same-sex marriages take issue with their cell-phone carrier having gay and lesbian people working for them? Did they care that their entertainment subscriber services, like DirecTV and Comcast, employed homosexuals? Did they also cancel their mobile phone or cable services because they did?

Did they care if World Vision employed gluttons?

The answer to these rhetorical questions are, of course, *no*. But to have a Christian organization open its doors and hire believers in Jesus Christ who are in same-sex marriages to help the organization fulfill its mission of helping hurting and forgotten children around the world apparently crossed their spiritually-acceptable line. How would having self-identified, Christian gay men and women working as employees to promote the ministry of World Vision negatively affect their work?

It wouldn't.

Speaker and author Melanie Deal wrote about the irony of dropping these child sponsorships and the message being sent to the children who had been rejected. "Because I have a doctrinal disagreement with fellow Christians, I'm choosing to break off my relationship with you. You can no longer count on my love and support because of the way I feel about some marriages in the U.S. staff. And I'm making this decision because of my devotion to Jesus!"[51]

She went on to address the sponsors who made that decision: "These kids aren't pawns. They've been victimized and exploited enough without Christians using them in some kind of epic doctrinal battle to the death. Everyone loses this battle. Mostly the kids."

"Christians, this isn't right. We can do better. When did following Jesus become about what we're against?"

Is this the message we want to communicate to the unsaved world? Is deciding to abandon more than three thousand innocent children an example of the inconsistency driving away an entire generation from the church and Jesus Christ?

Did this decision by Jesus's followers to turn their backs on thousands of impoverished children make Jesus proud, or embarrassed because His name was associated with it? It certainly seemed motivated by the same moral and spiritual superiority, or pride, exemplified by the Pharisees.

Did it make Him mad?

Food for Thought:

As you have read about the life of Christ on earth in the Bible:

1. Do you believe Jesus still gets mad?
2. What do you think Jesus would have said if He had been interviewed by CNN after the religious right came out so strongly against World Vision's decision?

ELEVEN

WDJD?
(What Did Jesus Do?)

IN CHAPTER 9, I reflected on two actions of what I believe fairness in the church looks like: consistency and reading God's Word with integrity, meaning taking the whole of what it says and not cherry-picking the snippets of Scripture that support what we want it to say. I'm confidant a third action should include modeling the life of Christ. Jesus is our example, so we ought to be looking closely at the biblical accounts that depict His attitude and treatment toward the marginalized in the Jewish world of His day. As His followers, we will then be able to reflect Him with confidence in our actions and attitude toward the marginalized in the world of our day.

Jesus made His mission clear: "For the Son of Man came to seek and save those who are lost" (Luke 19:10).

His life was about reaching out to those identified in the Jewish culture as sinners. As such, the religious leaders of His day criticized Him about associating with such *scum*. Here is how Jesus responded to one of their judgments:

> Later, Matthew invited Jesus and his disciples to his home as dinner guests, along with many tax collectors and other disreputable sinners. But when the Pharisees saw this, they asked his disciples, "Why does your teacher eat with such scum?" When Jesus heard this, he said, "Healthy people don't need a doctor—sick people do." Then he added, "Now go and learn the meaning of this Scripture: 'I want you to show mercy, not offer sacrifices.' For I have come to call not those who *think* they are righteous, but those who know they are sinners." (Matthew 9:10–13, emphasis added)

Jesus quoted from Hosea 6:6 when he challenged the religious leaders to learn the meaning of, "I want you to show mercy, not offer sacrifices." In the Old Testament, the word for *mercy* can be translated as "love" or "compassion"[52] When the Pharisees challenged Jesus about hanging out with disreputable sinners, His response was to remind them that God has always been about showing mercy, love, and compassion to those people recognized in their culture as "scum" because of their sinful lifestyles.

In the same way, I believe Jesus is asking the twenty-first century, North American church to go and learn the meaning of, "I want you to show mercy, not offer sacrifices." His desire is for His bride to respond with mercy, love, and compassion to the marginalized gay community and other *undesirables.*

Luke tells of another instance where Jesus was again challenged by the religious leaders:

> Tax collectors and other notorious sinners often came to listen to Jesus teach. This made the Pharisees and teachers of religious law complain that he was associating with such sinful people—even eating with them! So Jesus told them this story: "If a man has a hundred sheep and one of them gets lost, what will he do? Won't he leave the ninety-nine others in the wilderness and go to search for the one that is lost until he finds it? And when he has found it, he will joyfully carry it home on his shoulders. When he arrives, he will call together his friends and neighbors, saying, 'Rejoice with me because I have found my lost

sheep.' In the same way, there is more
joy in heaven over one lost sinner who
repents and returns to God than over
ninety-nine others who are righteous
and haven't strayed away!" (Luke
15:1–7)

There are a couple of points I want to make
regarding this passage. First, and I can't emphasize
this point enough, these *notorious sinners* came of
their own volition to hear Jesus teach and even
share a meal with Him. Just like the worst of sinners
felt comfortable, and were even drawn to be in the
presence of Jesus, homosexuals should not only feel
comfortable in the church, but also drawn to it.

Second, Jesus equated the tax collectors and
sinners with the one sheep that left His flock. This
one lost sheep He is talking about wasn't a member
of the church who stopped showing up to services
because of the god of recreation or the mattress de-
mon that wouldn't let them go on Sunday morning, although it could be. No, in this discussion
Jesus is saying the one lost sheep was one of the notorious sinners He ate with, who had not yet made
the decision to follow Him—the unsaved.

If Jesus were in our churches today, He would
leave (the other ninety-nine) in search of a marginalized person, such as a gay or lesbian, to rescue and

restore their relationship with the living God. Jesus considered even the most sinful to be His sheep, and part of His flock He loves so dearly.

WDJD?

He spent time with those the church alienated because they were considered the worst of sinners.

It's Hard to Hate Someone Up Close

In 1979 Jerry Falwell launched the political action committee, The Moral Majority. During the 1980s, it became one of the largest lobby groups representing the evangelical Christian right and was largely responsible for bringing Christian voters to support Ronald Reagan in his bid for the presidency in 1980. One of the targets of The Moral Majority was pornography, and for Jerry Falwell, the face of pornography was Larry Flynt, founder and publisher of Hustler magazine.

Falwell publicly referred to Mr. Flynt as a "sleaze merchant hiding behind the first amendment." *Hustler* retaliated by publishing a parody ad in 1983 insinuating Falwell had sex with his mother. This so infuriated Falwell, he brought a $45 million lawsuit against Flynt and *Hustler* in 1984.

Falwell won a $150,000 judgment in the initial trial, but to the surprise of many, the U.S. Supreme Court rendered a unanimous decision in a 1988 appeal in favor of Larry Flynt and *Hustler* magazine.

Nine years after the Supreme Court decision, radio and television personality Larry King hosted these two archenemies on his program. Even though they had starkly differing views, Jerry Falwell seemed to have softened and came across as friendly toward Larry Flynt.

Shortly after the episode, Falwell showed up unannounced at the offices of *Hustler* to see Flynt, who then invited him in. They talked for two hours, and Falwell suggested they tour the country debating moral and first amendment issues, which Flynt agreed to do.

Fast-forward to May 20, 2007, one week after Jerry Falwell's death. Larry Flynt published an article in the *Los Angeles Times* describing his relationship with Falwell after that meeting.

> In the years that followed and up until his death, he'd come to see me every time he was in California. We'd have interesting philosophical conversations. We'd exchange personal Christmas cards. He'd show me pictures of his grandchildren. I was with him in Florida once when he complained about his health and his weight, so I suggested that he go on a diet that had worked for me. I faxed a copy to his wife when I got back

home. My mother always told me that no matter how repugnant you find a person, when you meet them face to face you will always find something about them to like."

Flynt ended the article with this statement:

"The ultimate result was one I never expected and was just as shocking a turn to me as was winning that famous Supreme Court case: We became friends."[53]

The Moral Majority viewed *Hustler* magazine as an instrument of sleaze, degradation, and sin. *Hustler* magazine saw The Moral Majority as an enemy of the first amendment. But after the publisher of the one organization met and spent time with the president of the other organization, and put a face to the name, they saw each other as friends. We can do that too.

Let's do what Jesus did to reach the homosexual community and the marginalized: just hang out with them—spend time with them. When we do, we'll learn to love them. We need to look for opportunities to cross the line of hatred and judgment created by the bride of Christ, and express friendship and love in practical ways. If Jerry Falwell and Larry Flynt can overcome their differences and develop a genuine friendship, certainly we can do the same.

What does that look like practically?

1. **Reach out to those in the homosexual community God has already placed around us.**

Maybe ask that neighbor or coworker out for a cup of coffee and get to know him or her as a person—one who Jesus loves with His whole heart—a creation of God whom Jesus endured the savagery of the cross for so they could be in relationship with Him too.

2. **Approach him or her as a person and not a project.**

They can tell the difference, and this is a point I want to emphasize. Your motive should be to build a relationship with them and express Christ's love to them; to show them the kindness of God. As Theodore Roosevelt said, "They won't care how much you know, until they know in their heart how much you care."[54]

3. **Earn their trust.**

After you've gained their trust, just like in any friendship, they will want to know why you are different than the other Christians who would have nothing to do with them. Then you can share with them the story of how Jesus once searched for you as His one, lost sheep to restore you into the loving relationship with God you were created to have. You can share how God has loved them their whole life and wants that same relationship with them— just as they are.

4. Invite them to church.

There are some in the church who believe we shouldn't welcome homosexuals until they change. This is contrary and inconsistent to how we treat all the other unsaved people we reach out to. It is our job to introduce them to the person of Jesus, not to change them to get them ready for that introduction. We are called to love them, and we need to allow Christ to do the changing: "the riches of His kindness and tolerance and patience" are much greater than ours (Romans 2:4 NASB). In other words, we are not the Holy Spirit; we are ambassadors for Christ (2 Corinthians 5:20).

How Did Jesus Treat Homosexuals Specifically?

We don't have an absolute answer to that question, but I believe that by studying the life of Christ we can know with some degree of certainty what His actions would have looked like.

One of my favorite stories in the New Testament is found in John. The religious leaders brought a woman caught in adultery before Jesus and asked Him what should be done with her. They were trying to trap Him because they expected Him to say something contrary to Jewish law.

Deuteronomy gives clear instruction as to what was to be done with a woman caught in adultery: "If a man is discovered committing adultery, both he and the woman must die. In this way, you will purge Israel of such evil" (Deuteronomy 22:22).

I'm not sure where the man she had committed adultery with was, but under God's Law, the woman caught in adultery deserved to die. Instead, Jesus responded outside of the box when He confronted the crowd and said:

> "Let the one who has never sinned throw the first stone!" Then he stooped down again and wrote in the dust. When the accusers heard this, they slipped away one by one, beginning with the oldest, until only Jesus was left in the middle of the crowd with the woman. Then Jesus stood up again and said to the woman, "Where are your accusers? Didn't even one of them condemn you?" "No, Lord," she said. And Jesus said, "Neither do I. Go and sin no more." (John 8:7–11)

While we don't have a clear understanding of how the capital punishment of stoning was carried out two thousand years ago, Deuteronomy 13:9 seems to indicate the witness to the crime, or perhaps even the aggrieved—such as the wife of the man who committed adultery—would be responsible for throwing the first stone. After the first stone was thrown, then the rest of the crowd would join in to carry out the sentence of death.

Jesus knew once that first stone was thrown, the woman would be dead. So, Jesus gave the condition that the one to throw the first stone should be the one without sin. Only one thing prohibited the crowd from carrying out the prescribed Old Testament sentence—their own conviction that none of them were without sin.

But there was one person in the crowd who was without sin—Jesus. He was the only one in the mob who met the standard, and could have cast the first stone—but instead he pardoned her. Jesus's answer to the situation wasn't judgment and condemnation. Instead, He responded with grace and an affirmation of God's love for her. Jesus's response wasn't an attempt to abolish the Law, but to emphasize His life and presence in humanity that ushered in a change. He brought in the age of Jubilee—an age that no longer focused on judgment but, rather, on love and grace. The grace they all needed because everyone in that crowd was as guilty of breaking the Law as she was.

What if we changed the story a little bit?

What if instead of a woman caught in adultery, the religious leaders brought a young man caught having sexual relations with another man? The requirement of the Law was the same: death. Both sins fall under the category of *sexual immorality, impurity, lustful pleasures.* Take a moment to really think about the answer to this next question:

Would Jesus's response have been any different toward the young man?

I'm convinced beyond a shadow of a doubt, the answer to that question is a resounding *no*.

As Matthew West sang about in Grace Wins, we are in a war between guilt and grace, and the good news is, Jesus showed us that grace wins every time.

Focus on What's Truly Important

I think if we could learn to focus on what is truly important to God, we can begin to understand the other facets of the homosexuality issue and perhaps discover a different starting point for reaching the LGBTQ community—not their sin, but God's love for them. Paul wrote about this exact thing in his letter to the Galatians.

What is important is faith expressing itself in love. For you have been called to live in freedom, my brothers and sisters. But don't use your freedom to satisfy your sinful nature. Instead, use your freedom to serve one another in love. *For the whole law can be summed up in this one command: Love your neighbor as yourself.* (Galatians 5:6, 13, emphasis added)

Peter expressed similar thoughts, "Most important of all, continue to show deep love for each other, for love covers a multitude of sins" (1 Peter 4:8).

In these few verses, two biblical authors who were responsible for establishing the doctrine of the early church give us the *Cliff's Notes* for Christian living: "The most important thing of all is showing and expressing love." Period.

John writes, "Your love for one another will prove to the world that you are my disciples" (John 13:35).

Really? Does the homosexual community know us by our love? Probably not. They more likely know us by our judgmental attitudes, and I believe that breaks the heart of God.

If I haven't convinced you yet that gays and lesbians are not our enemy, then listen to the words of Jesus: "Love your enemies!" (Matthew 5:44, Luke 6:27, 35).

Why? Because Paul encourages us that "love never fails" (1 Corinthians 13:8).

I believe if we as the church are going to err on this issue, we should err on the side of love and follow the role model of grace that Jesus's life exemplified. As followers of Christ, we should be known by every human life we come into contact with by our love.

Are we?

Maybe it's time for the church to recognize, just like the crowd surrounding the adulterous woman did, that we are all as guilty of the Law as the homosexual person. Jesus was the only one in that murderous mob who had the right to judge and condemn, but He chose not to do so.

So, then, what right do we have?

We need to let the verbal and attitudinal stones we are so ready to throw at this marginalized segment of society—human beings Jesus created, died for, and loves with all His heart—drop from our hands to the ground, so that our hands will be free to reach out and embrace them, welcome them through our doors, and love them on the inside for who they are.

Let me leave you with one final thought:

"Christ Jesus came into the world to save sinners—and I am the worst of them all" (1 Timothy 1:15).

So am I.

What about you?

Works Cited

"11 Facts About Global Poverty," Dosomething.org, accessed July 12, 2020, https://www.dosomething.org/us/facts/11-facts-about-global-poverty.

"20 Inspirational Theodore Roosevelt Quotes," Dose of Leadership, accessed July 12, 2020, https://www.doseofleadership.com/20-inspirational-theodore-roosevelt-quotes/.

"2000 California Proposition 22," Wikipedia, accessed July 12, 2020, https://en.wikipedia.org/wiki/2000_California_Proposition_22.

Adam Nicholas Phillips, "The Wreckage of World Visions' LGBT Reversal Two Years Later," *Huffpost*, last modified December 6, 2017, https://www.huffpost.com/entry/the-wreckage-of-world-visions-lgbt_b_9551570?guccounter=1.

"Addiction & Industry: Pornography Statistics," Archomaha.org, accessed July 20, 2018, http://archomaha.org/wp-content/uploads/2015/09/Pornography-Statistics.pdf.

"Adult Obesity Facts," Centers for Disease Control and Prevention, accessed July 12, 2020, https://www.cdc.gov/obesity/data/adult.html.

Alan Manning Chambers, "Exodus Int'l President to the Gay Community: 'We're Sorry,'" Alan Chambers, accessed July 12, 2020, https://alanchambers.org/exodus-intl-president-to-the-gay-community-were-sorry/.

Amelia Thomson-DeVeaux, "Millennials Leave Their Churches Over Science, Lesbian & Gay Issues," PRRI, last modified October 6, 2011, https://www.prri.org/spotlight/millennials-leave-their-churches-over-science-lesbian-gay-issues/.

Ben Horowitz, "Rutgers student forced to care for siblings after parents were killed in Hurricane Sandy," NJ.com, last modified March 30, 2019, https://www.nj.com/news/index.ssf/2012/11/rutgers_student_forced_to_care.html.

"Billy Graham's Answer: What is Sin? Are All Sins Equal in God's Eyes?" Billy Graham Evangelistic Association, last modified March 26, 2014, https://billygraham.org/story/billy-grahams-answer-what-is-sin-are-all-sins-equal-in-gods-eyes/.

Brycchan Carey, "John Wesley's Thoughts upon slavery and the language of the heart," accessed July 12, 2020, https://www.brycchancarey.com/Carey_BJRL_2003.pdf.

"Centennial Olympic Park Bombing," Wikipedia,

accessed July 12, 2020, https://en.wikipedia. org/wiki/Centennial_Olympic_Park_bomb-ing.

"Christian Views on Slavery," Wikipedia, accessed July 12, 2020, https://en.wikipedia.org/wiki/ Christian_views_on_slavery#cite_note-96.

C.S. Lewis, "Mere Christianity," Novels77.com, accessed July 15, 2020, https://novels77.com/ mere-christianity/chapter-18-136460.html.

Daniel Burke, "Millennials Leaving Church in Droves, Study Finds," cnn.com, last mod-ified May 14, 2015, https://www.cnn. com/2015/05/12/living/pew-religion-study/ index.html.

Daniel Cox, Robert P. Jones, "Generations at Odds: The Millennial Generation and the Fu-ture of Gay and Lesbian Rights," PRRI, last modified August 29, 2011, https://www.prri. org/research/generations-at-odds/.

"Defining Adult Overweight and Obesity," Centers for Disease Control and Prevention, accessed July 12, 2020, https://www.cdc.gov/obesity/ adult/defining.html.

Elwood Watson, "Pornography Addiction Among Men Is on the Rise," *Huffpost*, last modified December 9, 2014, https://www.huffington-post.com/elwood-d-watson/pornography-ad-diction-amo_b_5963460.html.

"Firm Believers More Likely to Be Flabby, Purdue Study Finds," *Purdue News*, accessed July 12, 2020, https://www.purdue.edu/uns/html4ever/1998/9803.Ferraro.fat.html.

Frank Magdelyns, "Justitia," accessed July 12, 2020, photograph, https://pixabay.com/photos/justitia-lady-court-lady-justice-2673647/.

"Herd Mentality," Wikipedia, accessed July 12, 2020, https://en.wikipedia.org/wiki/Herd_mentality.

Jana Riess, "Why Millennials Are Really Leaving Religion (It's Not Just Politics, Folks)," *RNS Religion News Service*, June 26, 2018, https://religionnews.com/2018/06/26/why-millennials-are-really-leaving-religion-its-not-just-politics-folks/.

"Jeffrey Dahmer," Wikipedia, accessed July 12, 2020, https://en.wikipedia.org/wiki/Jeffrey_Dahmer#Arrest.

John Piper, "Are All Sins Equal Before God?" Desiring God, last modified November 9, 2009, https://www.desiringgod.org/interviews/are-all-sins-equal-before-god.

"Jubilee (and Sabbatical) Years," swcs.com, accessed July 12, 2020, https://www.swcs.com.au/jubilees.htm.

Larry Flynt, "Larry Flynt: My Friend, Jerry Falwell," *LA TIMES*, last modified May 20, 2007, https://www.latimes.com/la-op-flynt-20may20-story.html.

M. Goeke, "Why Homosexuality IS Different—the Reality," The Message, accessed July 12, 2020, https://baptistmessage.com/why-homosexuality-is-different-the-reality/.

"Materialistic," Thesaurus.com, accessed July 12, 2020, https://www.thesaurus.com/browse/materialistic?s=t.

"Matthew Poole's Commentary," BibleHub, accessed July 12, 2020, https://biblehub.com/commentaries/poole/isaiah/64.htm.

Mark Abshier, "Homosexuality and the church," Christian Chronicle, accessed July 15, 2020, https://christianchronicle.org/homosexuality-and-the-church/.

Maya Rhodan, "Christian Group That Flip-Flopped on Gay Marriage Loses Donors," TIME, last modified March 28, 2014, https://time.com/41918/christian-group-that-flip-flopped-on-gay-marriage-loses-donors/.

Mel White, Stranger at the Gate: To Be Gay and Christian in America, (Plume, 1995).

Melanie Dale, "World Vision, Gay Marriage, and Breaking Off Sponsorship," unexpected.org, last modified March 25, 2014, https://www.unexpected.org/2014/03/world-vision-gay-marriage-and-breaking-off-sponsorship/.

Michael Lipka & David Masci, "Where Christian Churches, Other Religions Stand on Gay Marriage," last modified July 2, 2015, https://www.

pewresearch.org/fact-tank/2015/12/21/where-christian-churches-stand-on-gay-marriage/.

"Obesity and Overweight," Centers for Disease Control and Prevention, accessed July 12, 2020, https://www.cdc.gov/nchs/fastats/obesi-ty-overweight.htm.

"Obesity in the Body of Christ," *The Courier*, last modified February 20, 2008, https://baptist-courier.com/2008/02/obesity-in-the-body-of-christ/.

"People who live in glass houses shouldn't throw stones," *Cambridge Dictionary*, accessed July 12, 2020, https://dictionary.cambridge.org/us/dictionary/english/people-who-live-in-glass-houses-shouldn-t-throw-stones.

"Richard Jewell," Wikipedia, accessed July 12, 2020, https://en.wikipedia.org/wiki/Richard_Jewell.

Ronald j. Ostrow, "Richard Jewel Case Study," Co-lumbia.edu, last modified July 13, 2000, http://www.columbia.edu/itc/journalism/j6075/edit/readings/jewell.html.

Roy Ratcliff, *Dark Journey Deep Grace: Jeffrey Dahmer's Story of Faith,* (Abilene, Texas: Leaf-wood Publishers, 2006), 161-62.

"Sacramento Baptist Pastor Praises Orlando Massa-cre," ABC 10 Connect, accessed July 12, 2020, https://www.abc10.com/article/news/local/

sacramento/sacramento-baptist-pastor-praises-es-orlando-massacre/243211965.

Sam Allberry, *Is God Anti-Gay?* (The Good Book Company, 2013).

"Say What? Origins of Words and Sayings," Origins of Sayings, last modified August 11, 2006, https://originsofsayings.blogspot.com/2006/08/people-who-live-in-glass-houses-should.html.

Henry Schuster, "I helped make Richard Jewell famous—and ruined his life in the process," The Washington Post, last modified December 6, 2019, https://www.washingtonpost.com/outlook/i-helped-make-richard-jewell-famous--and-ruined-his-life-in-the-process/2019/12/06/c3c205ec-177f-11ea-9110-3b34ce1d92b1_story.html.

Scott Freeman, "Presumed Guilty," *Atlanta Magazine*, last modified December 1, 1996, https://www.atlantamagazine.com/great-reads/presumed-guilty/.

T.F. Team, "A Horrific Account of Jeffrey Dahmer's Apartment as the Police Found It," Forensic Outreach, accessed July 20, 2018, https://forensicoutreach.com/library/a-horrific-account-of-jeffrey-dahmers-apartment-as-the-police-found-it/.

Terry Goodrich, "Portly Pastors Widespread, but

Sabbaticals and Peer Support Can Help Fight Fat, Baylor Study Finds," Baylor Media Communications, last modified January 12, 2015, https://www.baylor.edu/mediacommunications/news.php?action=story&story=150843.

Tom Rath, *StrengthsFinder 2.0* from (New York: Gallup Press, 2007), 77.

Wesley Hill, *Washed and Waiting: Reflections on Christian Faithfulness and Homosexuality.* (Zondervan on Brilliance Audio, 2016).

Philip Yancey, "Homosexuality," accessed July 12, 2020, https://philipyancey.com/q-and-a-topics/homosexuality.

Endnotes

Introduction

1 Ben Horowitz, "Rutgers student forced to care for siblings after parents were killed in Hurricane Sandy," NJ.com, last modified March 30, 2019, https://www.nj.com/news/index. ssf/2012/11/rutgers_student_forced_to_care. html.

2 Tom Rath, *StrengthsFinder 2.0* from (New York: Gallup Press, 2007), 77.

3 Rath, *StrengthsFinder 2.0*, 77.

4 Frank Magdelyns, "Justitia," accessed July 12, 2020, photograph, https://pixabay.com/photos/justitia-lady-court-lady-justice-2673647/.

5 "2000 California Proposition 22," Wikipedia, accessed July 12, 2020, https://en.wikipedia. org/wiki/2000_California_Proposition_22.

Chapter 1

6 Brycchan Carey, "John Wesley's Thoughts upon slavery and the language of the heart," accessed July 12, 2020, https://www.brycchan-carey.com/Carey_BJRL_2003.pdf.

7   "Christian Views on Slavery," Wikipedia, ac-
     cessed July 12, 2020, https://en.wikipedia.org/
     wiki/Christian_views_on_slavery#cite_note-
     96.

8   "Christian Views on Slavery."

Chapter 2

9   Michael Lipka & David Masci, "Where Chris-
     tian Churches, Other Religions Stand on Gay
     Marriage," last modified July 2, 2015, https://
     www.pewresearch.org/fact-tank/2015/12/21/
     where-christian-churches-stand-on-gay-mar-
     riage/.

10   M. Goeke, "Why Homosexuality IS Dif-
     ferent—the Reality," The Message, accessed
     July 12, 2020, https://baptistmessage.com/
     why-homosexuality-is-different-the-reality/.

Chapter 3

11   "Jeffrey Dahmer," Wikipedia, accessed July
     12, 2020, https://en.wikipedia.org/wiki/Jef-
     frey_Dahmer#Arrest.

12   T.F. Team, "A Horrific Account of Jeffrey
     Dahmer's Apartment as the Police Found It,"
     Forensic Outreach, accessed July 20, 2018,
     https://forensicoutreach.com/library/a-horrif-
     ic-account-of-jeffrey-dahmers-apartment-as-
     the-police-found-it/.

13 Roy Ratcliff, *Dark Journey Deep Grace: Jeffrey Dahmer's Story of Faith,* (Abilene, Texas: Leafwood Publishers, 2006), 161-62.

14 Elwood Watson, "Pornography Addiction Among Men Is on The Rise," Huffpost, last modified December 9, 2014, https://www.huffingtonpost.com/elwood-d-watson/pornography-addiction-amo_b_5963460.html.

15 Watson, "Pornography Addiction Among Men Is on The Rise."

16 "Addiction & Industry: Pornography Statistics," Archomaha.org, accessed July 20, 2018, http://archomaha.org/wp-content/uploads/2015/09/Pornography-Statistics.pdf.

17 7 "Defining Adult Overweight and Obesity," Centers for Disease Control and Prevention, accessed July 12, 2020, https://www.cdc.gov/obesity/adult/defining.html.

18 "Obesity and Overweight," Centers for Disease Control and Prevention, accessed July 12, 2020, https://www.cdc.gov/nchs/fastats/obesity-overweight.htm.

19 "Firm Believers More Likely to Be Flabby, Purdue Study Finds," Purdue News, accessed July 12, 2020, https://www.purdue.edu/uns/html4ever/1998/9803.Ferraro.fat.html.

20 "Obesity in the Body of Christ," The Courier, last modified February 20, 2008, https://bap-

tistcourier.com/2008/02/obesity-in-the-body-of-christ/.

21 "Adult Obesity Facts," Centers for Disease
    Control and Prevention, accessed July 12,
    2020, https://www.cdc.gov/obesity/data/adult.
    html.

22 Terry Goodrich, "Portly Pastors Widespread,
    but Sabbaticals and Peer Support Can Help
    Fight Fat, Baylor Study Finds," Baylor Media
    Communications, last modified January 12,
    2015, https://www.baylor.edu/mediacom-
    munications/news.php?action=story&sto-
    ry=150843.

Chapter 4

23 "Sacramento Baptist Pastor Praises Orlando
    Massacre," ABC 10 Connect, accessed July 12,
    2020, https://www.abc10.com/article/news/
    local/sacramento/sacramento-baptist-pas-
    tor-praises-orlando-massacre/243211965.

Chapter 5

24 John Piper, "Are All Sins Equal Before God?"
    Desiring God, last modified November 9,
    2009, https://www.desiringgod.org/inter-
    views/are-all-sins-equal-before-god.

25 "Billy Graham's Answer: What is Sin? Are
    All Sins Equal in God's Eyes?" Billy Graham

Evangelistic Association, last modified March 26, 2014, https://billygraham.org/story/billy-grahams-answer-what-is-sin-are-all-sins-equal-in-gods-eyes/.

26 "Materialistic," Thesaurus.com, accessed July 12, 2020, https://www.thesaurus.com/browse/materialistic?s=t.

27 "11 Facts About Global Poverty," Dosome-thing.org, accessed July 12, 2020, https://www.dosomething.org/us/facts/11-facts-about-global-poverty.

28 "Say What? Origins of Words and Sayings," Origins of Sayings, last modified August 11, 2006, http://originsofsayings.blogspot.com/2006/08/people-who-live-in-glass-hous-es-should.html.

29 "People who live in glass houses shouldn't throw stones," Cambridge Dictionary, ac-cessed July 12, 2020, https://dictionary.cam-bridge.org/us/dictionary/english/people-who-live-in-glass-houses-shouldn-t-throw-stones.

Chapter 6

30 Philip Yancey, "Homosexuality," accessed July 12, 2020, https://philipyancey.com/q-and-a-topics/homosexuality.

31 Alan Manning Chambers, "Exodus Int'l Pres-ident to the Gay Community: 'We're Sorry,'"

Alan Chambers, accessed July 12, 2020,
https://alanchambers.org/exodus-intl-presi-
dent-to-the-gay-community-were-sorry/.

Chapter 7

32 Ronald j. Ostrow, "Richard Jewel Case Study,"
Columbia.edu, last modified July 13, 2000,
http://www.columbia.edu/itc/journalism/
j6075/edit/readings/jewell.html.

33 "Richard Jewell," Wikipedia, accessed July 12,
2020, https://en.wikipedia.org/wiki/Richard_
Jewell.

34 "Centennial Olympic Park Bombing," Wikipedia, accessed July 12, 2020, https://en.wiki-
pedia.org/wiki/Centennial_Olympic_Park_
bombing.

35 Scott Freeman, "Presumed Guilty," Atlanta
Magazine, last modified December 1, 1996,
https://www.atlantamagazine.com/great-reads/
presumed-guilty/.

36 Henry Schuster, "I helped make Richard
Jewell famous—and ruined his life in the
process," The Washington Post, last modified December 6, 2019, https://www.
washingtonpost.com/outlook/i-helped-make-
richard-jewell-famous--and-ruined-his-life-
in-the-process/2019/12/06/c3c205ec-177f-
11ea-9110-3b34ce1d92b1_story.html.

37 "What is Sanctifying Grace," Got Questions,
    Accessed August 29, 2020 https://www.
    gotquestions.org/sanctifying-grace.html

38 "Matthew Poole's Commentary," BibleHub,
    accessed July 12, 2020, https://biblehub.com/
    commentaries/poole/isaiah/64.htm.

Chapter 8

39 "Jubilee (and Sabbatical) Years," swcs.com, ac-
    cessed July 12, 2020, https://www.swcs.com.
    au/jubilees.htm.

Chapter 9

40 Daniel Burke, "Millennials Leaving Church
    in Droves, Study Finds," cnn.com, last
    modified May 14, 2015, https://www.cnn.
    com/2015/05/12/living/pew-religion-study/
    index.html.

41 Jana Riess, "Why Millennials Are Real-
    ly Leaving Religion (It's Not Just Politics,
    Folks)," RNS Religion News Service, June 26,
    2018, https://religionnews.com/2018/06/26/
    why-millennials-are-really-leaving-reli-
    gion-its-not-just-politics-folks/.

42 Amelia Thomson-DeVeaux, "Millennials
    Leave Their Churches Over Science, Lesbian
    & Gay Issues," PRRI, last modified October
    6, 2011, https://www.prri.org/spotlight/mil-

lennials-leave-their-churches-over-science-les-
bian-gay-issues/.

43 42 Daniel Cox, Robert P. Jones, "Generations
at Odds: The Millennial Generation and the
Future of Gay and Lesbian Rights," PRRI, last
modified August 29, 2011, https://www.prri.
org/research/generations-at-odds/.

44 Cox, Jones, "Generations at Odds: The Millennial Generation and the Future of Gay and
Lesbian Rights."

45 Amelia Thomson-DeVeaux, "Millennials
Leave Their Churches Over Science, Lesbian
& Gay Issues."

46 45 "Herd Mentality," Wikipedia, accessed
July 12, 2020, https://en.wikipedia.org/wiki/
Herd_mentality.

Chapter 10

47 C.S. Lewis, "Mere Christianity," Novels77.
com, accessed July 15, 2020, https://novels77.
com/mere-christianity/chapter-18-136460.
html.

48 Adam Nicholas Phillips, "The Wreckage
of World Visions' LGBT Reversal Two
Years Later," Huffpost, last modified December 6, 2017, https://www.huffpost.
com/entry/the-wreckage-of-world-vi-
sions-lgbt_b_9551570?guccounter=1.

49 Maya Rhodan, "Christian Group That Flip-Flopped on Gay Marriage Loses Donors," TIME, last modified March 28, 2014, https://time.com/41918/christian-group-that-flip-flopped-on-gay-marriage-loses-donors/.

50 Maya Rhodan, "Christian Group That Flip-Flopped on Gay Marriage Loses Donors."

51 Melanie Dale, "World Vision, Gay Marriage, and Breaking Off Sponsorship," unexpected.org, last modified March 25, 2014, https://www.unexpected.org/2014/03/world-vision-gay-marriage-and-breaking-off-sponsorship/.

Chapter 11

52 "What Is Mercy? Bible Verses and Meaning," Christianity.com, Accessed August 30, 2020 https://www.christianity.com/wiki/christian-terms/what-is-mercy-why-is-it-important.html

53 Larry Flynt, "Larry Flynt: My Friend, Jerry Falwell," LA TIMES, last modified May 20, 2007, https://www.latimes.com/la-op-flynt-20may20-story.html

54 "20 Inspirational Theodore Roosevelt Quotes," Dose of Leadership, accessed July 12, 2020, https://www.doseofleadership.com/20-inspirational-theodore-roosevelt-quotes/.

Order Information

To order additional copies of this book, please visit
www.redemption-press.com.
Also available on Amazon.com and
BarnesandNoble.com
or by calling toll-free 1-844-2REDEEM.

CPSIA information can be obtained
at www.ICGtesting.com
Printed in the USA
LVHW030658160321
681657LV00009B/154

9 781646 450787